Nausea and Vomiting

Dr. Musarrat Ali
Dr. Sharique Zohaib

Made with ♥ on the Notion Press Platform
www.notionpress.com

NAUSEA & VOMITING
An Integrated Approach to Care

By
Dr. Musarrat Ali
MD *(Unani)* NIUM
Assitant Professor Dept. of Ilmul Saidla (Unani Pharmacy)
Mohammadia Tibbia College & Assayer Hospital Malegaon

&

Dr. Sharique Zohaib
MD *(Ilmul Advia)* MTC
Associate Professor & HOD of Dept. of *Ilmul Saidla* (Unani pharmacy)
Mohammadia Tibbia College & Assayer Hospital Malegaon

DEDICATED
TO
MY FATHER (ANWAR HUSAIN) MY FAIMLY
&
MY TEACHERS AND FRIENDS

PREFACE

The practice of *Unani* medicine is based on the basic principles of *Akhlat* (humors), *Mizaj* (temperament), etc. which explain by eminent *Unani* physicians. In this book we tried to explain the concept of Nausea & vomiting, their causes, history taking, clinical examination, and the addition to detailed line of treatment in cases of Nausea & Vomiting. The firm foundation of *Unani* concept will help the physicians in arriving at a provisional diagnosis and for planning relevant necessary investigations to confirm the diagnosis. This book is dedicated to the community of medical students whose thirst for knowledge make the teachers learn. Learning helps in the proper management of patients, Medicine is an ever changing science. The vast clinical experience, the technological advancement in the field of investigatory modalities, tremendous explosion in the invention and addition of newer drugs in the field of pharmacology, and a wide variety of interventional therapeutic advancements have contributed to the voluminous growth of medical literature. Human brain cannot remember all the facts. It is impossible to learn, register, Remember and to recall all the medical facts in the course of time bound undergraduate and postgraduate medical education.

It is the realization of these difficulties that prompted me to write this book. Hence, an earnest attempt has been made to merge the clinical methods and the principles of *Unani* medicine and to present both in a condensed form. To explain the *Unani* concept and literature about Nausea and Vomiting an Integrated Approch to care was the maintheme of this book. This book intended primarily for medical undergraduates and also for postgraduate hospital doctors, particularly those studying for higher clinical examinations or returning to clinical practice. The book is also an essential reference for *Unani* practitioners.

Dr. Musarrat Ali
Assistant Professor
Mohammadia Tibbia
College & Assayer
Hospital Malegaon

CONTENTS

ACKNOWLEGMENT

All praises be to "Almighty Allah" the lord of the world, the most beneficent and merciful and peace be upon his Prophet Mohammed (SAWS). Through the grace of Almighty Allah, the uphill task has been accomplished.

Foremost I would like to express my deep sense of gratitude to my beloved Grandparents and My Parents. For their Support and Guidance. I pray to Allah to show mercy to them and forgive them. I greatly appreciate the constructive suggestions and help that we have received from past and present friends, colleagues and focus groups in the design and content of the book. I Thankfull to my Guide **Dr. Sharique Shamsi**, Lecturer, Dept. of Ilmul saidla, National Institute of Unani Medicine, Bengaluru, for their collaboration.

I am thankfull to my teacher **Dr. Rashid Qazi Sir** Principal M.I.J Tibbiya Unani Medical College, Mumbai for there unconditional moral support. I would like to express my eternal and deep sense gratitude to **Maolana Arshad Mukhtar saheb**, Chairman Mohammadia Tibbia College Mansoora Malegaon. I also express my sincere gratitude to **Dr. Abdul Majid Katthe Wale,** CEO, Mohammadia Tibbia college, Malegaon for their throughout support. I am thankfull to **Dr. Sayyad Minhaj sir, Dr Abul Irfan Sir, Dr Saheda Rahemani madam and Dr sharique zohaib sir**, Head of Department *Ilmul Saidla*, Mohammadia Tibbia College for their collaboration in this work. Lastly thanks to my friends, **Dr Shahzad Amir, Dr. Abuzar lari, Dr. Zaid Iqbal, Dr Ifra, Dr Gufran, Dr Taj,** and **Dr. Ansari Mushir**. I always obliged to him for his support and cooperation, and their suggestion.

INTRODUCTION OF *UNANI* MEDICINE

The Unani System of Medicine is a medical system that deals with the management of health and diseases. It provides preventive, promotive, curative and rehabilitative healthcare with holistic approach. The fundamental framework of this system is based on deep philosophical insights and scientific principles, including the Empedoclean theory of four Elements I.e. Air, Water, Fire and Earth; four proximate Qualities (*Kayfiyat*) i.e. Hot, Cold, Wet and Dry described by Pythagoras, and the Hippocratic theory of four Humours (*Akhlat*) – Blood (*Dam*), Phlegm (*Balgham*), Yellow Bile (*Ṣafra*) and Black Bile (*Sawda*). Admixture of different Elements and their Qualities in specific ratio in a particular entity, whether living or non-living, denominates its Temperament (*Mizaj*). Human Temperament is commonly denoted by the dominant Humour i.e. Sanguine (Damawī), Phlegmatic (*Balghami*), Choleric (*Ṣafrawi*) and Melancholic (*Sawdawi*), which can be correlated with the Temperament of Diet, Drugs, Environmental Factors etc. as the entities of non-human Universe being made up directly of Elements are described in terms of Qualitative Temperament. Any disturbance in the equilibrium of humours causes disease, and therefore the treatment aims at restoring the equilibrium by giving factors (including drugs) of opposite temperament. In addition, Unani System of Medicine believes that Medicatrix naturae (*Ṭabi'at Mudabbira'-I Badan*) is the supreme power, which controls all the physiological functions of the body, provides resistance against the diseases and helps in healing naturally. The Unani System of Medicine is holistic in nature and takes into account the whole personality rather than taking a reductionistic approach towards disease. Unani physicians give prime importance to diet and the state of digestion in a person, in both health and disease. Specific dietary regimens are recommended while treating patients according to their temperament. Proper diets are assumed to produce good humours (*Akhlat Ṣaliḥa*) while improper ones produce bad humours (*Akhlat Radiyya*). Thus, the humoral imbalance can be corrected by medication coupled with proper diet. The physician prescribes the drugs according to the temperament of patient, causative humour, faculty of organ involved and severity of the disease. These drugs are classified as per the specific temperament (*Mizaj*) and are graded in the first, second, third and fourth degree according to their potency. The Unani System of Medicine offers treatment of diseases related to all the systems and organs of the human body. The treatments for chronic ailments and diseases of skin, liver, musculo-skeletal and reproductive systems, immunological and lifestyle disorders have been found to be highly effective and acceptable. The use of elatives, exhilarants, aphrodisiacs, organ-specific tonics and immunomodulatory drugs, temperament specific drugs, correctives for adverse effects, coctives and purgatives etc. are unique features of Unani System of Medicine. Cosmoceutics, Nutraceutics, Aromatics and corresponding therapies are important parts of treatment in Unani System of Medicine

Introduction of Nausea and Vomiting

(Qai and *Ghasiyan)*

(Summurized)

As per the concept of Unani System of Medicine (USM), vomiting can be defined as the movement of stomach for elimination of gastric content through mouth. The matter of vomiting always found in gastric cavity (*Jof-e-meda*). According to *Hakeem Mohammad Azam Khan,* author of *Akseer-e-Aazam* and *Hakeem Mohammad Kabeerudeen,* author of *Alakseer* and *Shaikh Ibne Sena* author of *Alqanoon-Fi-tibb,* retching (*Tahu or Ubkai*) is a movement of stomach to eliminate the content of stomach, but unable to eliminate it from mouth. The only difference between nausea and vomiting is that, in vomiting the matter expel out through mouth, while in nausea it is not expelled. The matter of nausea is found in tissues of stomach and patient feels pain and tenderness in stomach. *Ghasiyan or Matli* is a condition in which stomach tries to expel out the unwanted matter which is adheres to it without any movement. According to *Abul Hasan Ahemad bin Tabri,* author of *Al moaljat-e-buqaratiya Ghasiyan* or *matli* is a condition occurs before vomiting it may reveal earlier or may persist for a long time, if the causative matter of *ghasiyan* founds in stomach, then the disease persists for long time and if it falls from other organ then it reveals early. *Ghasiyan* occurs due to accumulation of foul smelling excessive matter and liquid. The matter of nausea is found in tissues of stomach and patient feels pain and tenderness in stomach.

According to *Atibba-e-qadeem*, Causes of nausea, vomiting and retching have similar causes, which is as follows, ulceration, irritation , tenesmus of stomach, improper dieting, collapse of stomach, renal colic, sever myalgia, hypersensitivity, hepatobiliary colic, uterine disease , cerebral trauma, abnormal humour, unwanted matter, spoiled food, food poisoning, weakness of stomach, gastric disease like inflammation of gastric mucosa, gastric ulcer, gastric carcinoma, atony of stomach, spasticity of stomach etc. Associated cause due to other disease cause activation of repulsive forces due to neurine stimulation, abdominal pain, Hepatobiliary pain, renal stone, cholilithiasis, inflammation of intestine, intestinal worms, cholecystitis, herniation, cardiac disorders, peritonitis, cirrhosis of liver, uterine disease, meningitis, brain tumour, coma, hysteria, ovarian disease, diabetes, infective fevers like small pox, chicken pox, measles etc. had vomiting in way of sequel of disease. Poisoning like Alcohol, Opium, Charas, Bhang, Arsenic, Tobacco, Lead, Mercury etc. ingestion or administration into blood stream causes vomiting.

As per the modern literature and Modern System of Medicine, vomiting is co-ordinated by the brain stem and is effected by neuro-muscular responses in the gut, pharynx, and thoraco-abdominal wall. The mechanisms underlying nausea are poorly understood but likely involve the cerebral cortex, as nausea requires conscious perception. Electro-encephalo-graphic studies show activation of temporo-frontal cortical regions with induction of nausea. Co-ordination of emesis Several brain stem nuclei initiate emesis including the nucleus tractus solitarius, the dorsal vagal and phrenic nuclei, and medullary nuclei that regulate respiration; nuclei that control pharyngeal, facial, and tongue movements co-ordinate the initiation of emesis. The neuro transmitters involved in this coordination are uncertain; however, roles for neurokinin NK1, serotonin, and vasopressin pathways are postulated. Somatic and visceral muscles exhibit stereotypic responses during emesis. Inspiratory thoracic and abdominal wall muscles contract producing high intra-thoracic and intra-abdominal pressures that facilitate expulsion of gastric contents. The gastric cardia herniates across the diaphragm, and the larynx moves upward to promote oral propulsion of the vomitus. Under normal conditions, distally migrating gut contractions are regulated by an electrical phenomenon, the slow wave which cycles at 3 cycles/min in the stomach and 11 cycles/min in the duodenum. With emesis, slow waves are replaced by orally propagating spike activity, which induces retrograde contractions that assist in the oral expulsion of small-intestinal contents.

In Modern System of Medicine most commonly used anti emetic agents act on the central nervous system. Anti-histamines such as meclizine and dimenhydrinate and anticholinergic drugs such as scopolamine act on labyrinthine-activated pathways and are useful in motion sickness and inner ear disorders. Phenothiazine and butyrophenone dopamine D2 antagonists are used to treat emesis evoked by area postrema stimuli and are effective for medication, toxic, and metabolic aetiologies. Dopamine antagonists freely cross the blood-brain barrier and may cause anxiety, dystonic reactions, hyper pro-lactinemic effects (galactorrhoea and sexual dysfunction), and irreversible tardive dyskinesia. Other drug classes have antiemetic properties. Serotonin 5-HT3 antagonists such as ondansetron and granisetron are useful in the treatment of post-operative vomiting, after radiation therapy, and in the prevention of cancer chemotherapy–induced emesis. The usefulness of 5-HT3 antagonists for other causes of emesis is less well stablished. Low-dose tricyclic antidepressants provide symptomatic benefit in patients with unexplained nausea of a functional nature, as well as in diabetic patients with nausea and vomiting whose disease is of long standing.

In Unani System of Medicine (USM), many single drugs such as *Sana* (Casia angustifolia), *Atees Shireen* (Aconitum hetrophyllum), *Heel khurd* (Elettaria cardamomam), *Anaar* (Punica grantum), *Doob* (Cynodon ductylan), *Nana* (Mentha viridis), *Heel Kalan* (Amomum subulatum), *Amla* (Emblica officinalis), *Papita* (Carica papaya), *Khas* (Andropogon muricatis), *Alocha* (Prunus avium), *bahi* (Cydonia oblongata), *Peepal* (Ficus religiosa), *Dhaniya* (Coriander sativum), *Zarishk* (Berperis vulgaris), *Tabasheer* (Bambusa spinose), *Lemo* (Citrus limon), *Narangi* (Citrus limon), *Post bairon-e-pista* (Pistaica vera), *Lattku* (Eriobotrya japonica), *Podina (*Mentha sylvestris), *Zaranbad* (Curcuma zedoaria) are used orally to treat nausea vomiting and retching. Formulations in different dosage forms are also used in nausea, vomiting and retching such as *Sharbat-e-Anaar, Sharbat-e-Hamaz, Sharbat-e-Hasram, Sharbat-e-Fataq, Sharbat-e-Khaskhas, Sharbat-e-Falsa,*

Sharbat-e-Ribas, Sharbat-e-Nilofar, Sharbat-e-Tamar Hindi, Sharbat-e-Limo, Sharbat-e-Sandal,

Jawarish-e-Anarain, Jawarish-e-Tamar Hindi, Safoof Tabasheer, Qurs Mastagi, Qurs Papita, Qurs Rasan, Qurs Kunder, Qurs Samaq, Qurs Khabsul Hadeed, Laoq-e-Annar dana, Rub-e-Bahi, Rub-e-Saeb Sada, Rub-e-Ribas, Rub-e-Hamaz, Khameera-e-Uood tursh, Khameera-e-Sandal Tursh, Sikanjabeen-e-Limoni, Habb-e- Zaranbad.

UNANI CONCEPT OF NAUSEA & VOMITING

As per the concept of Unani System of Medicine (USM), vomiting can be defined as the movement of stomach for elimination of gastric content through mouth. The matter of vomiting always found in gastric cavity (*Jof-e-meda*).

RETCHING (*Tahu, Ubkai*)

Retching (*Tahu or Ubkai*) is a movement of stomach to eliminate the contemt of stomach but unable to eliminate it from mouth. The only difference between nausea and vomiting is, in vomiting the matter expel out through mouth while in nausea it is not. The matter of nausea is found in tissues of stomach and patient feels pain and tenderness in stomach.

NAUSEA (*Ghasiyan or Matli*)

Ghasiyan or Matli is a condition in which stomach tries to expel out the unwanted matter which is adhere to it without any movement. *Ghasiyan* or matli is a condition occurs before vomiting. It may reveal earlier or may persist for a long time, if the causative matter of *ghasiyan* founds in stomach then the disease persists for long time and if it falls from other organ then it reveals early. *Ghasiyan* occurs due to accumulation of foul smelling excessive matter and liquid[4]. The matter of nausea is found in tissues of stomach and patient feels pain and tenderness in stomach.

CAUSES OF NAUSEA AND VOMITING

Nausea and vomiting have similar causes, which is as follows: ulceration, irritation, tenesmus of stomach, improper dieting, collapse of stomach, renal colic, sever myalgia, hypersensitivity, hepatobiliary colic, uterine disease, cerebral trauma, abnormal humour, unwanted matter, spoiled Food, food poisoning, weakness of stomach, gastric disease like inflammation of gastric mucosa, gastric ulcer, gastric carcinoma, atony of stomach, spasticity of stomach etc. Associated cause due to other disease cause activation of repulsive forces due to neurine stimulation, abdominal pain, cholilithiasis, inflammation of intestine, intestinal worms, cholecystitis, herniation, cardiac disorders, peritonitis, cirrhosis of liver, meningitis, brain tumour, coma, hysteria, ovarian disease, diabetes, Infective fevers like small pox, chicken pox, measles etc. Poisoning like alcohol, opium, chars, bhang, arsenic, tobacco, lead, lercury etc.

TYPES OF NAUSEA AND VOMITING

1) Nausea and vomiting of bile (*Safrawi Qai wa Matli*)

In this type of vomiting the patient feels burning sensation and thrust, the vomitus contains bitter biliary Humour.

2) **Nausea and vomiting of bhlegam** *(Bulgami Qai or Matli)*

In this type of vomiting and nausea is due to phlegmatic matter.

3) **Nausea and vomiting of black bile** *(Saudavi Qai wa matli)*

In this type the vomitus contains black bile.

4) Aqueous and Acidic vomiting and nausea *(Rutoobi and Humuzi Qai wa Matli)*

In aqueous and acidic vomiting, there is absence of burning and thrust but the patient feels flatulence and crackling sound in abdomen. The vomitus is bitter.

Vomiting due to crises (*Bohran*)

In case of crises the vestigial or abnormal matter comes to the stomach which is expelled out through vomiting.

5) Hematemesis (*Qai-u-Dam*)

In hematemesis there is blood in vomitus due to trauma to vessels or abrasion, opening of ends of vessels or contusion to stomach.

6) Vomiting due to infection (*Ufooni Qai wa Matli*)

It occurs due to infectious matters which is accumulated in stomach.

7) Vomiting due to worms (*Qai e Didani*) It is due to intestinal worms.

SIGN AND SYMPTOMS OF NAUSEA AND VOMITING

(*Alamat e Qai wa Matli*)

1) *Phlegmatic* symptoms with crackling sound and flatulence appear when the cause of vomiting and nausea is excessive liquid and acidity. *Phlegmatic* taste also feels by patient.
2) Burning in abdomen and excessive thrust are the symptoms when the cause is bile. In this case taste of vomitus is bitter. Relevant symptoms appear accordingly when the cause is due to other disease.
3) If vomiting occurs after one and half hours of food, it shows that the cause is in stomach.
4) If it occurs after 2-3hrs then may be the cause is in the small intestine.
5) If after a long time, then the cause may be in large intestine.
6) In gastric, biliary and intestinal disease, vomiting is accompanied with nausea, if applied light pressure on stomach the patient feels pain.

DIAGNOSIS

In cerebral disorder, vomiting occurs due to increase body temperature and slight stimulation may cause vomiting, if apply pressure on stomach patient not feels pain and tenderness. While it is opposite in gastric, intestinal and hepatic disorder. The method of diagnosis of nausea and vomiting is that first rule out the involment of another disease like cholera, indigestion, abdominal pain, oesophageal ulcer, ulceration in gums, gastritis, hepatitis, inflammation of spleen, inflammation of kidney, intestinal worms, febrile illness. If nausea and vomiting are present with any other disease, then it is called complication of that disease. If it is not due to any other disease, then check out its continuously, if it is persisting then it is itself as disease. In this case ask the diet of patient before occurring of vomiting and if patient has history of taking spoiled food then the cause of vomiting is indigestion. You should check for the alteration in the temperament plain with matter (*Sue Mijaz sada maddi*) if symptom present and stomach trying to expel out its content than it confirms that the disease is due to *sue mizaj sada maddi*. If there is presence of symptom of *humours* then the cause behind it will be the *humours*.

Ilaj (Treatment Single Drugs)

The treatment of a medical disorder with a single drug is known as monotherapy or single drug therapy. In *Unani* system of medicine is term as *Ilaj bil mufradat*. In current era, we are observing that, to cure any disease or disorder the physician uses compound formulations for their patients instead of a single medicine. And no any doubt they cure the conditions quite successfully. It is proven that compound formulations are very effective to cure certain pathological conditions, but in this view the importance of single drugs are strictly not negligible. In fact, ancient *Unani* physicians highly recommended single drug therapy for managing any pathological condition. *Zakariya Raazi*, one of the ancient physician in Unani system of medicine has quoted that "whenever it is possible to treat by single drugs there is no need of compound formulations". Another ancient physician *Shaikh-ur-raees ibn-sina* also recommends single drug therapy over compound formulation. (Canon of medicine) Many single drugs such as *Sana* (Casia angustifolia), *Atees Shireen* (Aconitum hetrophyllum), *Heel khurd* (Elettaria cardamomam), *Anaar* (Punica grantum), *Doob* (Cynodon ductylan), *Nana* (Mentha viridis), *Heel Kalan* (Amomum subulatum), *Amla* (Emblica officinalis), *Papita* (Carica papaya), *Khas* (Andropogon muricatis), *Alocha* (Prunus avium), *bahi* (Cydonia oblongata), *Peepal* (Ficus religiosa), *Dhaniya* (Coriander sativum), *Zarishk* (Berperis vulgaris), *Tabasheer* (Bambusa spinose), *Lemo* (Citrus limon), *Narangi* (Citrus limon), *Post bairon-e-pista* (Pistaica vera), *Lattku* (Eriobotrya japonica), *Podina* (Mentha sylvestris), *Zaranbad* (Curcuma zedoaria)

ATEES SHIREEN

Aconitum heterophyllum

Drug *Atees* consists of dried, tuberous roots of *Aconitum heterophyllum* Wall ex. Royle of Ranunculaceae family. Drug yielding plant is a perennial herb, native of western Himalayas and found in Garhwal, Kumaon and Kashmir at altitude between 2500-4000m.

OTHER NAMES:

Arabic: *Atees*

Persian: *Atees, Vaj-e-Turki*

Assamese: Aatieh

Bengali: Ataieha

English: Indian Atees

Gujarati: Ativishni Kali ativikhani Kali, Atvasa, Ativish, Atavishnikali

Hindi: Atis, Atvika

Kannada: Athivisha, Athibage

Kashmiri: Hongisafed, Mohandiguj Safed

Malayalam: Atividayam, Ativitayam

Marathi: Ativisha, Atavish

Oriya: Atushi

Punjabi: Atisa, Atees, Bonga, Chitijari Sukhihasi

Sanskrit: Ativisha, Sitashringi Bangura, Pankura

Tamil: Ativadayam, Atividyam

Telegu: Ativasa, Ativasu

Urdu: *Atees*

CHEMICAL CONSTITUETNS:

Alkaloids (atisine, dehydroatisine, hetisine and heteratisine)

ACTION:

Daf-e-Humma, Qabiz, Habis-ud-Dam, Muqawwi-e-Meda, Moharrik-e-Asab.

THERAPEUTIC USES:

Zof-e-Meda, Qai, Ishal, Zaheer-e-Muzmin.

DOSE: 2 to 3 gm.

IMPORTANT FORMULATION:

Majoon-e-Joqraj Gugal

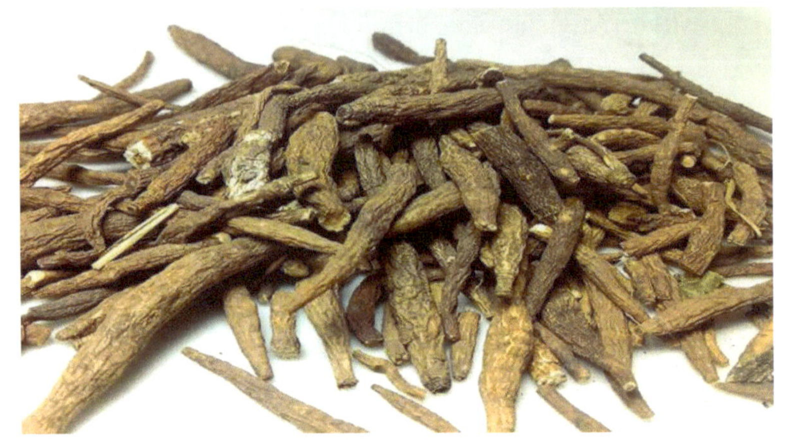

ATEES SHIREEN (*Aconitum heterophyllum*)

ATEES SHIREEN (*Aconitum heterophyllum*)

ANAR

Punica granatum

The drug *Anar* consists of fresh seeds of *Punica granatum* Linn. (Fam. Punicaceae), a large
deciduous shrub or a small tree; found growing wild in the warm valley, outer hills of Himalayas,
between 900- 1800 m and cultivated in many parts of the country.

OTHER NAMES:

Urdu: *Anar*
Arabic: *Rumman*
Persian: *Anar*, *Nar*
Bengali: Dadima
English: Pomegranate
Gujarati: Dadama
Hindi: *Anar*
Kannada: Dalimba
Malayalam: Matalam
Marathi: Dadimba
Punjabi: *Anar*
Sanskrit: Dadima
Tamil: Madalai, Maadalai. Madalam
Telugu: Danimma

CHEMICAL CONSTITUENTS:

Sugars, Vitamin C, Sitosterol, Ursolic acid, Protein,
Fat and Mineral matters, Nicotinic acid, Pectin,
Riboflavin, Thiamine, Delphinidin diglycoside, Aspartic,
Citric, Ellagic, Gallic and Malic acids, Glutamine,
Isoquercetin, Estrone and Punicic acid.

TEMPERAMENT:
Anar Shireen-Cold and Moist
Anar Tursh-Cold and Dry
ACTION:
Anar Shireen- *Muqawwi-e-Qalb* (Cardiac tonic),
Muqawwi-e-Jigar (Liver tonic), *Musakkin Atash*
(Allays'thirst), *Muwwalid-e-Dam* (Haematogenic),
Muddir-e-Baul (Diuretic)

Anar Tursh- *Qabiz* (Constipative)
Muqqawi-e-Qalb (Cardiac tonic), *Muqawwi-e-Jigar* (Liver Tonic),
Musakkine-e-
Safra (Bile sedative), *Musakkine-e-Dam* (Blood sedative), *Mudirre-e-baul*
(Diuretic)
Qat-e-Safra (Antibilious).

THERAPEUTIC USES:
Anar shireen*: Atash-e-Mufrit* (Polydipsia*), Zof-e-*
Am (General Weakness), Faqruddam (Anaeia),
Anar Tursh: *Sozish-e-Sadr* (Burning in the chest), *Ghasiyan*
(Nausea), *Qai* (Vomitting), *Yarqan* (Jaundice), *Atashe-*
Mufrit (Polydipsia).
DOSE: *Juice of Anar-* 25-60 ml
IMPORTANT FORMULATIONS:
Sharbat-e-Anar, Jawarish-e-Anarain, Jawarish-e- Pudina

Anar (Punica granatum)

MASTAGI (RESIN)

Pistacia lentiscus

The drug *Mastagi* is a resin obtained from *Pistacia lentiscus* Linn. (Fam. Anacardiaceae); a shrub or small tree indigenous to the countries bordering on the Mediterranean.

OTHER NAMES:

Urdu: *Mastagi*

Arabic: Mastakee, Alakkhmee, Ilkurumee, *Mastagi*

Persian: *Kundur Roomi*

English: Mastic

Hindi: *Rumi Mastagee, Rumi Mastiki, Mastagee*

 Bengali: *Rumi-Mastungi*

 Gujrati: *Rumi Mastagee*

Marathi: *Rumaa Mastakee*

CHEMICAL CONSTITUENTS:

Resin, volatile oil, a bicyclic terpenoid and fatty acids.

TEMPERAMENT:

Hot2° and Dry2°

 ACTION:

Muqawwie Meda wa Jigar, Kasire Riyah

THERAPEUTIC USES:

Zof-e-Meda, Zof-e-Jigar, Nafakh-e-Shikam. Qai (Vomiting)

DOSE: 1-2 gm

IMPORTANT FORMULATIONS:

Jawarish Mastagi, Jawarish Jalinoos

MASTAGI (RESIN) (*Pistacia lentiscus*)

MASTAGI (RESIN) (*Pistacia lentiscus*)

PAPITA

Carica papaya Linn.

Native to West Indies and Central America; now cultivated in Uttar Pradesh, Punjab, Rajasthan, Gujarat, Maharashtra and South India.

OTHER NAMES:

English: Papaya, Papaw.

Ayurvedic: Erand-karkati, Papitaa.

 Unani: Papitaa Desi.

Siddha/Tamil: Pappaali, Pappayi.

Action

 Ripe fruit—stomachic, digestive, carminative, diuretic, galactagogue.

THERAPEUTIC USES:

Useful in bleeding piles, haemoptysis, dysentery and chronic diarrhoea.

Seeds— emmengagogue, abortifacient, vermifuge. Juice of seeds is administered in enlarged liver and spleen, and in bleeding piles.

DOSE:

 Leaf—40–80 ml infusion; latex—3–6 gm

IMPORTANT FORMULATIONS:

Habb-e-Papita, Qurse e Papita

Papita (*Carica papaya* Linn.)

NANA (PUDINA)

Mentha viridis

The drug *Pudina* consists of the aerial part of *Mentha viridis* Linn. syn. M. spicata var. viridis Linn. (Fam. Lamiaceae) a perennial, creeping aromatic herb of 30 to 90 cm high, widely cultivated throughout the plains of India for culinary and medicinal purposes.

OTHER NAMES:

Urdu: *Pudina*

Arabic: *Fodanj, Naana*

Persian: *Pudina*

English: Spear-Mint, Garden Mint

Hindi: *Pudeenaa*

Bengali: *Pudinaa*

Gujrati: Phudino

Tamil: *Pudeenaa*

Marathi: *Pudinaa*

Punjabi: Parari pudina

Telugu: *Pudeenaa*

CHEMICAL CONSTITUENTS:

Essential oil (0.2 to 0.8 percent) containing terpene such as carvone (60%) and limonene (10%) as major constituents.

TEMPERAMENT:

Hot2° and Dry 2°

ACTION:

Munzij Mawade Ghaleez, Kasire Riyah, Muqawwie Meda, Mudirre Baul wa Tams, Musakkine Dard, Qatile Kirm, Daffe Taaffun.

THERAPEUTIC USES:

Zofe Meda, Nafakhe Shikam, Qai, Ehtabase Baul wa Tams, Ishale Atfal, Nafe Haiza.

DOSE:

3 - 5 gm

IMPORTANT FORMULATIONS:

Jawarish Pudina, Arq Pudina, Arq Ajeeb, Jawarish Anarain, Sikanjbeen Naanai

NANA (PUDINA) *(Mentha viridis)*

TAMAR HINDI
Tamarindus indica

The drug *Tamar Hindi* consists of fruit pulp without seeds of *Tamarindus indica* Linn. (Fam. Caesalpinaceae), a moderate sized to large evergreen tree upto 24 m in height and 7 m in girth, cultivated throughout India, or self sown in waste places and in forest lands; also planted as avenue tree.

OTHER NAMES:

Urdu: *Imli*
Assamese: Tamar, Teteli
Bengali: Tetula, Tentul, Ambli
English: Tamarind Tree
Gujarati: Anvali
Hindi: *Imli*
Kannada: Hunisemale
Malayalam: Puli, Amlam
Marathi: Chinch
Oriya: Koina, Omlika
Punjabi: *Imli*, Amli
Sanskrit: Amlika
Tamil: Puli, Aanvilam
Telugu: Chint, Chinta

CHEMICAL CONSTITUENTS:

Inorganic acids, Sugars, Saponin and bitter Principle-Tamarindinca

TEMPERAMENT:

Hot and *Moist*
ACTION:

Mus-hil-e-Safra (Bile Purgative), *Musakkin*
(Sedative)
THERAPEUTIC USES:
Atash-e-Mufrit (Polydipsia), *Ghasiyan* (Nausea),
Qai (Vomiting)
DOSE: 4-10 gm
IMPORTANT FORMULATIONS:
Jawarish-e-Tamar Hindi, Sikanjabeen Tamar Hindi

TAMAR HINDI (*Tamarindus indica*)

TAMAR HINDI (*Tamarindus indica*)

HEEL KHURD

Elettaria cardamomum

Drug *Heel Khurd* consists seeds of dried fruits of *Elettaria cardamomum* (Linn.) Maton and its varieties of Zingiberaceae family. Drug yielding plant is a stout large perennial herb, growing naturally in moist forests of western ghats up to 1500 m, also cultivated in many other parts of south India at an elevation from 750-1500 m.

OTHER NAMES:

Arabic: *Qaqla Sighar, Shamashar, Khairbua, Sho-Shmir*

Persian: Khair Buwa, Hel Buwa

Assamese: Sarooplakchi

Bengali: *Chota Elachi*, Garate

English: Cardamom

Gujarati: *Elchi*, Elaochi, Elayachi

Hindi: *Chhoti Ilayachi*

Kannada: Elakki, Sanna yalakki

Malayalam: Elam, Chittelam, Elakka ya

Marathi: Velloda, Lahanveldoda, Velchi

Oriya: Gujarati Cholaa leicha, Olaicho, Ela

Punjabi: Illachi, Choti Ilachi

Sanskrit: Truti, Ela, Sukshmaila

Tamil: Elam, Elakaya; Ella-Kay

Telegu: Chinne Elakulu, Sanna Elakulu, Elakkaya, Pakkuln

Urdu: *Heel Khurd*

CHEMICAL CONSTITUENTS: Essential Oil

ACTION:

Muqawwi-e-Meda, Mutayyib-e-Dahan, Kasir-e-Riyah, Muffarreh, Musakkin, Muqawwi-e-Qabl.

THERAPEUTIC USE:

Bakhrul fam, Zof-e-Hazm, Nafkh-e-Shikam, Zof-eQalb, Khafqan, Qai, Ghisyan

DOSE: 0.5 to 1 gm.

IMPORTANT FORMULATIONS:

Jawarish-e-Anarain, Jawarish-e-Bisbasa, Jawarish-e-Jalinoos, Jawarish-e-Narmuskh, Jawarish-e-Ood Tursh, Jawarish-e-Pudina, Jawarish Shahi, Jawarish-e-Shahreyaran, Jawarish-e-Tamar Hindi, Jawarishe-Zanjabeel, Jawarish-e-Zarishk, Majoon-e-Azaraqi, Majoon-e-Dabeedul Ward, Majoon-e-Jalali, Majoone-Kalkalanaj, Majoon-e-Lana, Majoon-e-Mughalliz, Majoon-e-Kuluki, Majoon-e-Muqil, Majoon-e-Supari Pak, Majoon-e-Mufarreh Barid, Majoon-e-Mufarreh-e-Barid Jawahar Wali, Marham Raskapoor, Raughane-Babuna Qawi, Araq-e-Ambar, Araq-e-Heel Khurd, Araq-e-Juzam, Sufoof-e-Hazim-Kalan, Sufoof-e-Qaranful, Sufoof-e-Satt-e-Gilo,

HEEL KHURD *(Elettaria cardamomum)*

NARANGI

Citrus reticulate

The drug *sangtara* consist of rind of fruit *Citrus reticulate Blanco*.Syn. Citrus aurantium L. (Rutaceae); an evergreen bushy moderate sized tree; cultivated throughout India in plain and higher elevations fruits are globose or sub globose with thin tight or loos rind.

Others Name:

Arabic: *Naranj*

Persian: Narang

Bengali: Kamal lebu

English: Madarin, tangerine

Hindi: *Santara*

Kannad: Kittale

Kashmiri: Soh niamata

Malyalam: Madhura naranga

Marathi: Santara

Oriya: Kamala, Santra

Punjabi: Santara

Sanskrit: Airvata

Tamil: Kamala, Kudagu

Telgu: Kamalapandu

Urdu: *Narangi*

Chemical Constituents

Citromitin, Cholestrol, Citromitin, linalool, campesterol, Neohesperdine, α-terpinene, β-pinene, Terpindene, Sabinene, p-cymene, β-Sitosterol, Myrcene, α-teripieol, Dimethyl anthranilate.

Temprament:

Cold 2° Moist2°

Action:

Muqawwi-e-Qalab, Muqawwi-e-Meda, Dafe-Ufunat,

THERAPEUTIC USE:

Zof-e-Meda Dafe-Qai

DOSE: Q.S

IMPORTANT FORMULATIONS:

Safoof-e-sangtara

Narangi *(Citrus reticulate)*

SANA

Cassia angustifolia

Drug *Sana* consists of dried leaves of *Cassia angustifolia* Vahl. of Leguminosae family. Drug yielding plant is a small shrub, 60-70 cm high found throughout the year, cultivated largely in Southern India, especially in districts of Tinnevelly, Madurai and Tiruchirapally a has also been introduced in Mysore; fully grown, thick bluish colour leaves stripped off by hand, collected and dried in shade for 7-10 days, till assume a yellowish-green colour; graded and then packed into large bales.

OTHER NAMES:

Arabic: *Sana Makki*

Persian: *Sana*

Assamese: Sonamukhi

Bengali: Svarnamukhi, Sonpat, Sannamakki

English: Indian Senna, Tinnevelly Senna

Gujarat: Mindhiaval, Senamakhi, Nat-ki-Sana

Hindi: Sanaya, Hindisana

Kannada: Nelavarika, Nilavaka, Chinnukki, Adapatiyan

Marathi: Sonamakhi

Oriya: Shonamukhi

Punjabi: Sanapati, Sarnapatta, Sannamakhi

Sanskrit: Svarnapatri, Bhumiari, Bhupadama.

Tamil: Nilpponnai, Avarai, Nilavirai, Nilavagai,

Telgu: Sunamukhi, Nelaponna, Nelatengedyu.

Urdu: *Sena, Barg-e-Sana*

CONSTITUENTS:

Anthraquinone, Glucoside, Flavonoids, Steroids and Resin

ACTION:

Mushim, Munaqqi-e-Dimagh, Jali, Mufatteh Sudad, Mukhrij-e-Deedan-e-Ama, Musaffi-e-Dam, Daf-e-Qai

THERAPEUTIC USE:

Waj-ul-Mafsil, Waj-ul-Qntn, Waj-ul-Warik, Irq-un-Nisa, Niqras, Zeeq-un-Nafas, Jarab, Busoor, Qulanj

DOSE:

5 to 10gm.

IMPORTANT FORMULATIONS:

Habb-e-Shabyar, Majoon-e-Musaffi-e-Khoon, Majoon-e-Ushba, Sufoof-e-Chobchini, Sufoof-e-Lajward, Itrifal Ghudadi, Itrifal-e-Shahatra, Sufoof-e-Mulaiyin, Sufoof-e-Mushil.

(Sana -e -Makki) Cassia angustifolia

AAMLA

Emblica officianalis

Drug *Aamla* consists of pericarp of dried mature fruits of *Emblica officianalis* Gaertn. Syn. Phyllanthus emblica Linn. of Euphorbiaceae family. Drug is mostly collected in winter season after ripening and in kashmiri in summer. Drug yielding plant is a small or medium sized tree, found both in natural state in mixed deciduous forests of the country ascending to 1300 m on hills, cultivated in gardesn, homeyards of grown as a road side tree.

OTHER NAMES:

Arabic: *Amlaj*

Persian: *Aonla, Amla*, Amuleh, Amial

Assamese: Amlaku, Amlakhu, Amluki, Ambali, Sohmyrlain.

Bengali: Amla, Dhatri, Amlaki, Amlati

English: Emblic Myrobelan, Indian Goosebery

Gujarati: Ambala, Amala

Hindi: Amla, Aonla, Amlika,

Kannada: Nallika, Nelli, Amalaka, Nellikkai

Kashmiri: Ambali, Amli Aonla

Malayalam: Nellikka, Nellikai, Nelli

Marathi: Anvala, Avolkathi, Avala, Arda, Bhuiawali, Aonli

Oriya: Gondhona, Amlaki, Ahalu

Punjabi: Amla, Ambli, Ambal

Sanskrit: Dharti-phala, Amraphalam, Amalku, Adiphala

Tamil: Nellikkai, Nelli, Topi Amalagam

Telegu: Usirikayi, Nelli, Amalekamu, Usiri, Triphalam Usirikai

Urdu: *Aamla, Amlaj*

CHEMICAL CONSTITUENTS:

Ascorbic acid and gallo tannins

ACTION:

Muqawwi-e-Qalb, Qabiz, Musakkin, Muqawwi-e-Dimagh

THERAPEUTIC USE:

Zof-e-Dimagh, Nisyan, Suda, Qarha-e-Meda, Humuzat-e-Meda, Ishal Qai

DOSE: 3 to 5 gm.

IMPORTANT FORMULATION:

Anoshdaru, Murabba-e-Amla, Majoon-e-Maqawwi-e-Rahem, Majoon-e-Mundi, Majoon-e-Lana, Majoon-e-Kundur, Qurs-e-Mulaiyin Jawarish-e-Aamla Sada, Sufoof-e-Hazim Kalan, Dawa-ul-Misk Motadil Sada, Itrifal, Zamani, Itrifal-e-Sagheer, Itrifal-e-Ustu-Khuddus, Sufoof-e-Aamla.

Amla (Emblica officianalis)

TURANJ

Citrus medica

The drug *Turanj* consists of dried pericarp of *Citrus medica* Linn. (Rutaceae), an evergreen shrub, 1.8 to 3.6 m high, found wild in kumaon, panchmarhi, Sikkim, Garo Hills, Khasia Hills.

OTHER NAMES:

Arabic: *Utraj*

Persian: *Turanj*

Bengali: Bara Numbu, Begpura, Bijaura, Honsanebu, Lebu,

English: Citron

Gujarati: Bijora, *Turanj*

Hindi: Bara Nimbu, Bijapura

Kannada: Nallika, Nelli, Amalaka, Nellikkai

Kashmiri: Ambali, Amli Aonla

Malayalam: Gilam, Matalanarakam

Marathi: Limbu, Mahalunga, Mavalung

Punjabi: Bajauri, Nimbu

Sanskrit: Amlakeshara, Begapura,

Tamil: Kadarangai, Turunji

Telegu: Lungamu

Urdu: *Aamla, Amlaj*

CHEMICAL CONSTITUENTS:

Essential Oil

ACTION:

Daf-e-Qai (Antiemetic)

THERAPEUTIC USE:

Qai wa Ghishiyan (Nausea and Vomitng)

DOSE: 3 to 5 gm.

 IMPORTANT FORMULATION:

Anushdaru Lului Jawarish R Tamar Hindi, Jawrish Zarishk, Khamira e Abresham hakeem Arshad wala

Turanj *(Citrus medica)*

HEEL KALAN

Amomum subulatum

The drug *Heel Kalan* consists of dried seed of *Amomum subulatum* Roxb. (Fam Zingiberaceae); an herb with leafy stem and perenninal root stock; cultivated in swampy places along the sides of mountain streams in Bengal, Assam, Kernataka & Kerala.

OTHER NAMES:

Urdu: *Badi Elaichi*

Arabic: *Qaqila Kibar*

Persian: *Heel Kalan*

English: Greater or Nepal cardamom

Hindi: *Bari elachi*

Bengali: Baara aliach

Gujarati: Elaicho, Mothi Elichi.

Kannada.: Dodda Yalakki, Nepdi Elakki

Tamil: Periya elam, Baraelam, Kattu elam

Malayalam: Valiya Elam, Perelam

Marathi: Mothi elayachi

Oriya: Bada aleicha, Aleicha

Punjabi: Budi elechi

Telugu: Pedda Elakulu

CHEMICAL CONSTITUENTS: Volatile oil (rich in Cineole)

TEMPERAMENT:

Hot and *Dry*

ACTION:

Muqqawwi-e- Meda, Hazim, Kasir-e-Riyah, Mutayyeb-e-Dahan

THERAPEUTIC USES:

Zof-e-Meda, Zof-e-Hazm, Nafakh-e-Shikam, Bu-e-Dahan. Daf-e-Qai

DOSE: 500 mg – 1 gm

IMPORTANT FORMULATIONS:

Jawarish Anarain, Jawarish Bisbasa, Zaroor Katha, Safoof-e-Kath.

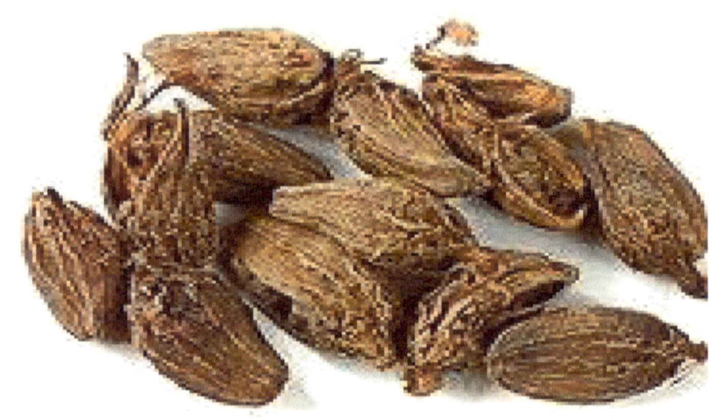

HEEL KALAN *(Amomum subulatum)*

HEEL KALAN *(Amomum subulatum)*

DOOB (Root)

Cynodon dactylon

The drug *Doob* consists of dried fibrous roots of *Cynodon dactylon* (Linn.) Pers. Syn. Panicum dactylon Linn. (Fam. Poaceae); an elegant, hard, perennial, creeping grass growing throughout the country and ascending to 2440 m.

OTHER NAMES:

Urdu: *Doob Ghas*, *Doob*

Arabic: *Ushb*

English: Creeping Cynodon, Couch Grass, Lawn Grass

Hindi: *Doob*

Bengali: Durva

Gujarati: Khadodhro, Lilidhro, Dhro

Kannad: Garike Hullu

Tamil: Aruvam Pullu

Malayalam: Koruka Pullu

Marathi: Doorva, Hariyalee, Harlee

Punjabi: Dubada

Telugu: Garika, Pacchgaddi

CHEMICAL CONSTITUENTS:

Phenolic Phytotoxins and Flavonoids.

TEMPERAMENT: Moderate towards cold.

ACTION:

Musakkin-e-Meda, Musakkin-e-Hararat, Mudirre-e-Baul.

THERAPEUTIC USES:

Surkh Bada, Shara, Sozish-e-Baul, Qai.

DOSE: 3-5 gm

DOOB (Root) *Cynodon dactylon*

DOOB (Root) *Cynodon dactylon*

***KHAS* (Root)**

Vetiveria zizanioides

The drug *Khas* consists of dried fragrant fibrous roots of *Vetiveria zizanioides* (Linn.) Syn. *Phlaris zizanaides* Linn. Nash (Fam. Poaceae); a densely tufted grass, found throughout the plains and lower hills of the country, especially on the banks of rivers and rich marshy soil, ascending to an altitude of 1200 m.

OTHER NAMES:

Urdu: *Khas*

Arabic: *Khas*

Persian: *Khas*

English: Cuscus Grass

Hindi: Khasa, Gandar, Bena, *Khas*

Bengali: Venarramula, Khaskhas

Gujarati: Sugandhi Valo, Valo

Kannad: Mudivala, Baladaberu, Lamanch, Bala Daberu

Tamil: Vetiver, Vilamichaver

Malayalam: Ramaceam, Vetiver, Lamajja, Ramacham

Marathi: Bala, Vala

Oriya: Ushira, Benachera

Punjabi: Panni, Khas

Telugu: Vetivelu, Vettiveru

CHEMICAL CONSTITUENTS:

Essential oil**.**

TEMPERAMENT: Cold and Dry

ACTION:

Mufarreh Qalb, Muqawwi-e-Qalb, Muqawwi-e-Dimagh, Daf-e-Safra, Ghasayan, Muqawwi-e-Meda, Musakkin-e-Atsh.

THERAPEUTIC USES:

Khafaqan, Zof-e-Qalb, Zof-e-Meda. Qai

DOSE: 5-7 gm

IMPORTANT FORMULATION:

Sharbat-e-Khas, Itr-e-Khas

KHAS (**Root**) (*Vetiveria zizanioides*)

BIHIDAANAA

Cydonia oblonga Mill

Synonym *C. vulgaris Pers.* Family Rosaceae. Habitat Cultivated in Punjab, Kashmir and the Nilgiri hills.

OTHER NAMES:

English: Quince Fruit.

Ayurvedic Amritaphala, Paatalaa, Simbitikaa.

Urdu: Bihi, Bihidaanaa.

Tamil: Shimaimathala.

CHEMICAL CONSTITUENTS: Glycoside, Amygdalin, Tannin, Mucilage

Action

Demulcent; used in irritable bowel syndrome, diarrhoea, dysentery, constipation, and in irritable conditions of the mucous membrane. Astringent.

THERAPEUTIC USES:

Irritable bowel syndrome, Diarrhoea, Dysentery, Constipation, Anti-Emetic

DOSE:3-9gm

IMPORTANT FORMULATION:

Banadiq-ul-Buzoor, Habb-e-Shaheeqa, Laooq Behidana, laooq sapistan

Bihidaanaa *(Cydonia oblonga)*

LOKAAT

Eriobotrya japonica

Habitat Native to China; now cultivated mainly in Saharanpur, Dehradun, Muzaffarnagar, Meerut, Kanpur, Bareilly districts of Uttar Pradesh, Amritsar, Gurdaspur and Hoshiarpur districts of Punjab.

OTHER NAMES:

English Loquat, Japanese Medlar.

Ayurvedic Lottaaka (non-classical). Unani Lokaat.

Siddha Ilakotta, Nokkotta (Tamil).

CHEMICAL CONSTITUENTS: lipopolysaccharides (LPS), Maslinic and ursolic acids

Action Leaves—used in China and India for the treatment of diabetes mellitus and skin diseases.

Fruit— sedative, Antiemetic.

Flower— expectorant.

THERAPEUTIC USES:

Leaves—used in China and India for the treatment of diabetes mellitus and skin diseases. Fruit— sedative, Antiemetic. Flower— expectorant.

DOSE: 7-15gm

Lokat (Eriobotrya japonica)

ZARANBAD

Curcuma zedoaria

Zaranbad is a root of herb, which is similar to turmeric. It is dried after boiling called *kachor*. Root of *Zaranbad* is slightly larger than Ginger, colour and taste of *Zaranbad* is similar to Ginger, taste of *Zaranbad* is like ginger better. Outer colour of root is like clay and inner colour of *Zaranbad* root is pale yellow.

BOTANICAL NAME:
Curcuma zedoaria, Rosc.
Others Name:

English	:	Zedoary, Round Zedoary
Arabic	:	*Aurakula – kappura,* Araqul kafoor
Persian	:	*Kasherver, Zaranbad*
Sanskrit	:	*Kachura, Sati*
Hindi	:	*Gandamasti, Kakhur, Kachura, Kali Haldi*
Urdu	:	*Zaranbad*
Unani	:	*Zaranbad*
Ayurvedic	:	*Kachura, Karchura, Draavida, Palashi, Gandhmuulaka, Shati*
Telugu	:	*Kachuram, Kichchiligaddalu*
Malayalam	:	*Pulan-Kizhanna*
Bengali	:	*Ekangi, Kachura*
Spanish	:	Cedoaria

German : Zitwer

Chinese : Er-Jyur

French : Zedoaire

PART USED:

Root, Rhizomes and Leaves, Tubers and Leaves

TEMPERAMENT:

Har Yabis 2^0 (Hot & Dry 2^0)

Medicinal Use:

Habis-e-Qai (Anti-Emetic)

THERAPEUTIC DOSE: 5-7 grams

IMPORTANT FORMULATION:

Safoof-e-chutki, *Habb-e-kabid Naushadri, Habb-e-Zaranbad, Majoon Murrawah-ul- Arwah, Majoon Nishara-i-Ajwali*, *Roghan-e-Surkh*, *Mufarreh Shaikh-ul- Rais*, *Mufarreh Motadil, Mufarreh Yaquti Motadil, Arq-e-Hazim*, *Majoon Chobchini, Majoon-e-Zaranbad.*

Zaranbad (*Curcuma zedoaria*)

COMPOUND DRUGS

Aims and Objectives to prepare *Murakkabat* (Compound Formulation)

There are following reasons for the use of compound formulations:

Unwanted effects:

A drug may be added to prevent unwanted effects of the drug, as in adding Peppermint (*Mentha pipperetta* herb) to Senna (*Cassia senna* leaf) to prevent cramping.

To reduce strength:

Compounding with drugs of opposite property may reduce excessive strength of drug.

Taste:

Distasteful drugs are prepared with those that improve their taste.

Enhance power:

Drug may be added to enhance or extend the time of action of the drug.

Corrective:

Drugs may destroy the harmful properties of a drug, as by mixing *Zafran* (Crocus sativa gynacium) with *Afiun* (Papaver somniferum Linn latex). Some drugs have property of toxic or poisonous side effects themselves. In such cases, a compound is prepared that neutralize toxic effects.

Inadequate:

Sometimes a single drug is simply inadequate.

Effective use:

Sometimes in order to use a drug effectively, it is necessary to mix it with ingredients, as in adding oil and wax to powdered drugs to use as an ointment.

To suppress unwanted action:

Sometimes there is a variance between the action of the drug and the nature of the disease, as when a single drug works in opposite actions at the same time, like ripening *phlegm* and hindering the growth of tumors. One would compound in order to avoid aggravating one or the other of these conditions, since the desire is to treat them in sequence, not at the same time.

Sue Mizaj **(Imbalance of temperament):**

Reason for preparation compound drug concerns the extent of the imbalance of the *humour* that is, if there is no single drug with enough force to restore balance, it is compounded with others that are stronger (or weaker) in the component desired. Thus, the tendency of the *humour* to continue in the direction of further imbalance is opposed.

Site of action:

The affected parts of body may be far from the site of administration, and drugs are mixed into the compound that speeds the drug to the site of action.

Synergistic action:

The strength and acuteness of the illness may be such that no single drug is sufficient against it. The drugs are mixed so that the ingredients have a synergistic action and effect.

Disease strength:

The strength and importance of the diseased organ must be taken together. Usually a drug to dissolve a tumor is compounded with one to ease the symptoms.

There is always a difference between drugs, their doses and usage. Sometimes the effects of both may be desired.

ARQ-E-ILAICHI

Definition:

Arq-e-Ilaichi is a liquid preparation obtained by distillation of ingredients in the formulation composition given below:

Formulation composition:

1. *Ilaichi Khurd*   *(Elettaria cardamomum)*   280 gm

2. *Ilaichi Kalan*   *(Amomum subulatum)*   350 gm

3. *Aab Sadah*   (Purified water)   12.Lit.

Method of preparation:

- Take all the ingredients of pharmacopoeial quality.

- Clean and dry the ingredients 1 and 2 under shade.

- Crush Ilaichi Khurd and Ilaichi Kalan in an iron mortar to obtain coarse powder.

- Soak the coarse powder of Ilaichi Khurd and Ilaichi Kalan in water overnight.

- Transfer the soaked powder along with water into distillation plant.

- Distil the soaked material to get 7.5 Lit. of Arq.

Actions

Muqawwi-e-Meda (Stomachic), *Mufarreh* (Exhilarant)

Therapeutic uses:

Zof-e-Meda (Weakness of stomach), *Haiza* (Cholera) *Daf e Qai*

Dose

75ml twice daily

Mode of administration

The drug is taken orally along with *Sharbat-e-Leemu* or alone.

ARQ-E-NANA

Definition:

Arq-e-Nana is a liquid preparation obtained by distillation of the ingredients in the quantity given below.

Formulation composition:

1. *Pudina Sabz*   *(Mentha arvensis)*   500 g

2. *Sirka desi*   (Vinegar)   8.0 Lit.

Method of preparation:

Clean the *Pudina Sabz* by washing it with purified water. Cut the *Pudina Sabz* into small pieces. Soak it in *sirka desi* in the flask of distillation plant. Distil the soaked material to get 6 lit of *Arq.* Collect and store the distillate in tightly closed containers to protect from light and moisture.

Therapeutic uses:

Qai (Vomiting), and *Zof-e-Hazm* (Dyspepsia)

Actions:

Muqawwi-e-Meda (Stomachic).

Dose: 80 ml

Mode of Administration:

The drug can be taken orally with *Sikanjbeen*

SHARABAT-E-ANAAR

Definition:

It contains pomegranate as its main ingredient and is known for its cooling and refreshing properties.

Formulation composition:

Aabe Anar Shirin	*(Punica granatum)*	1kg
Qand Safed	(Sugar)	1kg

Method of preparation:

To make *sharbat e aanar*, first make a juice of *anaar*.

Place in a stainless steel pan and heat (there will be some scamming, which can be taken off as it cools). Prepare *Qiwam* (Basic Solution of Particular consistency). Cool and store for later use.

Therapeutic uses:

Diarrhoea, excessive thirst, liver dysfunction, weakness of the liver, nausea and vomiting.

Dose:

Take 25 ml. with chilled water

Mode of Administration:

can be taken orally

SHARBAT-E-HAMAZ

Definition:

It contains *Hamaz* as its main ingredient and is known for its cooling and refreshing properties.

Formulation composition:

Aabe Hamaz		1.5lit.
Qand Safed	(Sugar)	1kg

Method of preparation: To make syrup, first make a *Decoction.*

Place in a stainless steel pan and heat (there will be some scamming, which can be taken off as it cools). Prepare *Qiwam* (Basic Solution of Particular consistency). Cool and store for later use.

Therapeutic uses:

Diarrhoea, excessive thirst, liver dysfunction, weakness of the liver, nausea and vomiting.

Dose:

Take 25 ml. with chilled water

Mode of Administration:

can be taken orally

JAWARISH-E-MASTAGI

Definition:

Jawarish-e-Mastagi is a semi-solid preparation made with the ingredients in the formulation composition given below:

Formulation composition:

1. *Mastagi*   (Pistacia lentiscus)   30 gm

2. *Arq-e-Gulab*   (Rosa damascena Mill)   200 ml

3. *Qand Safaid*   (Sugar)   500 gm

Method of preparation:

• Take all the ingredients of pharmacopoeial quality.

• Grind the ingredient number 1 in a porcelain mortar by slow and light motion and keep separately.

• Dissolve ingredient number 3 with ingredient number 2 in 200 ml of water on slow heat.

• Mix the 0.1% citric acid, while boiling and prepare quiwam of the 76% consistency.

• Remove the vessel from the fire and mix the powder of ingredient number 1, thoroughly and prepare the homogenous mass and allow it to cool.

Actions:

Muqawwi-e-Meda (Stomachic), *Kasir-e-Riyah* (Carminative)

Therapeutic uses

Zof-e-Meda (Weakness of the Stomach), *Sailan-e-Loab-e-Dahan* (Hypertyalism / Salivation), *Nafkh-e-Shikam* (Flatulence in the stomach) *Is-hal* (Diarrhoea)

Dose: 5-10 gm

Mode of administration with water

JAWARISH PUDINA WILAYTI

Definition:

Jawarish Pudina Wilayti is a semi-solid preparation made with the ingredients in the formulation composition given below:

Formulation composition:

1. *Berg Sudab*	*(Ruta graveolens)*	22 gm
2. *Boora* Armani	(Bole armeniac)	56 gm
3. *Zanjabeel*	*(Zingiber officinale)*	230 gm
4. *Zeera Safaid*	*(Cuminum cyminum)*	185 gm
5. *Zeera Siyah*	*(Carum carvi)*	375 gm
6. *Filfil Siyah*	*(Piper nigrum)*	175 gm
7. *Agar Hindi*	*(Aquilaria agallocha)*	7 gm
8. *Ilaichi Khurd*	*(Elettaria cardamomum)*	7 gm
9. *Ilaichi Kalan*	*(Amomum subulatum)*	7 gm
10. *Pudina Khushk*	*(Mentha arvensis)*	7 gm
11. *Taj Qalmi*	*(Cinnamomum cassia)*	7 gm
12. *Jaiphal*	*(Myristica fragrans)*	7 gm
13. *Qaranfal*	*(Syzygium aromaticum)*	7 gm
14. *Anardana*	*(Punica granatum)*	300 gm
15. *Tamar Hindi*	*(Tamarindus indicus)*	300 gm

16. *Maweez Munaqqa (Vitis vinifera)*   300 gm

17. *Qand Safaid*   (Sugar)   7.3kgm

18. *Sirka Desi*   (*Vinegar*)   450 ml

19. *Sat Pudina*   (Peppermint)   10 gm

20. *Sharbat Zanjabeel*   (*Zingiber officinale*)   1Lit.

21. *Aab-e-Leemun Lemon*   500 ml

Method of preparation:

• Take all the ingredients of pharmacopoeial quality.

• Clean, dry and powder the ingredients number 1 to 13 of the formulation composition separately and pass through a sieve of mesh number 80.

 • Clean and soak the ingredient number 14, 15 and 16 of the formulation composition for 3 h in 1000 ml of water.

• Then boil the content for 30 min on slow heat and cool it.

• Crush the ingredients and filter through muslin cloth and keep separately.

• Grind the ingredient number 19 of the formulation composition using mortar and pestle and keep separately.

• Mix the ingredient number 18, 20 and 21 of the formulation composition together and keep separately.

• Dissolve the specified quantity of ingredient number 17 (*Qand Safaid*) as per formulation composition in 500 ml extract of ingredient number 14, 15 and 16, add 1000 ml of water and boil on slow heat.

• At the boiling stage, add 0.1% citric acid and sodium benzoate and mix thoroughly to prepare the 70% consistency of *quiwam*.

• To this *quiwam* add the mixed ingredients 18, 20 and 21 and mix thoroughly.

• Then recorrect the *quiwam* to 80% of consistency.

• Remove the vessel from the fire.

• While hot add the mixed powdered ingredients 1 to 13 and mix thoroughly to prepare the homogenous product and allow it to cool.

Action

Muqawwi-e-Meda (Stomachic)

Therapeutic uses

Zof-e-Hazm (Indigestion), *Qai* (Vomiting), *Ghasiyan* (Nausea)

Dose 5 gm

Mode of administration The drug is taken orally.

JAWARISH-E-BISBASA

Definition:

Jawarish-e-Bisbasa is a semi-solid preparation made with the ingredients in the formulation composition given below:

Formulation composition:

1. *Heel Kalan*	*(Amomum subulatum)*	50 gm
2. *Bisbasa*	*(Myristica fragrans)*	30 gm
3. *Saleekha*	*(Cinnamomum cassia)*	30 gm
4. *Heel Khurd*	*(Elettaria cardamomum)*	30 gm
5. *Zanjabeel*	*(Zingiber officinale)*	30 gm
6. *Darchini*	*(Cinnamomum zeylanicum)*	30 gm
7. *Asaroon*	*(Asarum europaeum)*	30 gm
8. *Filfil Siyah*	*(Piper nigrum)*	20 gm
9. *Qaranfal*	*(Syzygium aromaticum)*	15 gm
10. Qand Safaid	(Sugar)	1000 gm

Method of preparation:

• Take all the ingredients of pharmacopoeial quality.

• Clean, dry and grind the ingredients number 1 to 9 separately and pass through sieve number 80.

• Dissolve ingredient number 10 and 11 in 1000 ml of water on slow heat.

• Mix the 0.1% citric acid, while boiling and prepare quiwam of 76% consistency.

• Remove the vessel from the fire. While hot condition, add powders of ingredients 1 to 9 and mix thoroughly to prepare the homogenous mass.

Actions

Muqawwi-e-Meda (Stomachic), *Kasir-e-Riyah* (Carminative), *Dafe-Qai* (Antiemetic)

Therapeutic uses

Zof-e-Meda (Weakness of the stomach), *Zof-e-Hazm* (Indigestion), *Bawaseer Amya* (Blind piles), *Nafkh-e-Shikam* (Flatulence in the stomach), *Ghasiyan* (Nausea)

Dose 5-10 gm

Mode of Administration with water

JAWARISH-E-ZANJABEEL

Definition:

Jawarish-e-Zanjabeel is a semi-solid preparation made with the ingredients in the formulation composition given below:

Formulation composition:

1. *Zanjabeel* (*Zingiber officinale*) 100 gm

2. *Samagh-e-Arabi* (*Acacia Arabica*) 50 gm

3. *Dana Heel* (*Elettaria cardamomum*) 50 gm

4. *Belgiri* (*Aegle marmelos*) 50 gm

5. *Saleekha* (*Cinnamomum cassia*) 25 gm

6. *Zarambad* (Curcuma zedoaria) 10 gm

7. *Nishashta-e-Gandum (Triticum aestivum)* 200gm

8. *Qand Safaid* (Sugar) 1.5 kg

Method of preparation:

• Take all the ingredients of pharmacopoeial quality.

• Clean, dry and grind the ingredients number 1 to 6 separately and pass through sieve number of mesh number 80.

• Take the required quantity of ingredient number 7 and keep separately.

- Dissolve the ingredient number 8 in 1000 ml of water on slow heat.

- Add 0.1% citric acid, while boiling, mix well and prepare the quiwam of 76% consistency.

- Remove the vessel from the fire.

- Add powders of ingredients 1 to 7 and mix thoroughly to prepare the homogenous mass and allow it to cool.

Actions:

Muqawwi-e-Ama (Intestinal tonic), *Muqawwi-e-Meda* (Stomachic), *Qabiz* (Costipative)

Therapeutic uses:

Is-hal (Diarrhoea), *Zof-e-Ishteha* (Anorexia), *Nafkh-e-Shikam* (Flatulence in the stomach)

Dose 5-10 gm

Mode of administration with water

JAWARISH-E-SAFRA SHIKAN

Formulation composition:

1. *Tamar Hindi*   *(Tamarindus indica)*   6 kg.

2. *Zanjabeel Khushk* *(Zingiber officinale)*   1 kg.

 3. *Qand Safaid*   (sugar)   18 kg.

Method of preparation:

Prepare *Zulal* of *Tamar Hindi*, Prepare *Qiwam* after adding sugar in it. Grind *Zanjabeel Khushk* finely and add it in the *Qiwam.*

Action:

Daf-e-Safra, Mufatteh Sudad

Therapeutic use:

Ghasiyan, Qai, Yarqan Suddi

Dose: 5 to 10gm

JAWARISH-E-TABASHEER QABIZ

Formulation composition:

1. *Tabasheer (Bambusa arundinasia)*	10gm
2. *Gul-e-Surkh (Rosa damascena)*	30gm
3. *Sumaq (Rhus coriaria)*	30gm.
4. *Gulnar Farsi (Punica Granatum)*	15gm
5. *Heel Khurd (Elettaria cardamomum)*	15gm
6. *Mastagi (Pistacia lantiscus)*	15gm
7. *Rubb-e-Behi (Cydonia oblongata)*	15gm
9. *Sharbat-e-Anar Tursh (Punica granatum)*	30ml

Action:

Hazim, Kasir-e-Riyah, Daf-e-Qai

Therapeutic use:

Zof-e-Meda, Nafkh-e-Shikam, Ghasiyan Dawar, Qai, Ishal.

Dose: 5 to 10 gm

JAWARISH TABASHEER

Its name is due to its chief ingredient *Tabasheer* (*Bambusa arundinasia* dried exudate on node)

Action:

Muqavvi Meda (Gastric tonic), prevents gases to be absorbed

Uses:

Qai (Vomiting), *Safravi Is-hal* (Biliary Diorrhoea)

Chief Ingredient:

Tabasheer (Bambusa arundinasia dried exudate on node)

Formulation composition:

Amla Muqashsher	*(Emblica officinalis)*	35gm
Gule Surkh	*(Rosa damascena)*	35gm
Kashneez Khushk	*(Coriandrum sativum)*	35gm
Sandal safed	*(Santalum album)*	35gm
Tabasheer	*(Bambusa arundinasia)*	35gm
Habbul Aas	*(Myrtus communis)*	35gm
Mastagi	*(Pistacia lantiscus)*	35gm
Post Simaq	*(Echinochloa)*	35gm
Post Turanj	*(Citrus medica)*	35gm
Kafoor	*(Cinnamomum camphora)*	5gm

Asl   (Honey) three times of all drug weight

Preparation: Make powder of all drugs and mix in *Qiwam* (Basic Solution of Particular consistency) of *Asl* (Honey).

Dose: 5-10gm

JAWARISH-E-TAMAR HINDI

Its name is due to its chief ingredient *Tamar Hindi (Tamarindus indica fruit pulp)*

Action:

Muqavvi Meda (Gastric tonic), *Muqavvi Qalb* (Cardiac tonic) and *Mushtahi* (Appetizer) Uses: *Safravi Qai* (Biliary vomiting), *Safravi Is-hal* (Biliary Diorrhoea) and *Matli* (Nausea)

Chief Ingredient:

Tamar Hindi (Tamarindus indica)

Formulation composition:

Tamar Hindi	*(Tamarindus indica)*	50gm
Gule Surkh	*(Rosa damascene)*	10gm
Kashneez	*(Coriandrum sativum)*	10gm
Berg Podina	*(Mentha arvensis)*	5gm
Dana Heel Khurd	*(Elettaria cardamomum)*	5gm
Mastagi	*(Pistacia lantiscus)*	5gm
Post Turanj	*(Citrus medica)*	5gm
Sandal safed	*(Santalum album)*	5gm
Sazij Hindi	*(Cinnamomum obtusifolium)*	5gm
Tabasheer	*(Bambusa arundinasia)*	5gm
Zarishk	*(Berberis aristata)*	5gm

Anar (*Punica granatum*)	1 in number
Murabba Amla	1 in number
Chini (Sugar)	more than three times of total drug

Preparation:

Get decanted solution of *Tamar Hindi* (*Tamarindus indica* fruit pulp). Make powder of powder able drugs and mix in decanted solution of *Tamar Hindi* (*Tamarindus indica* fruit pulp) mix in *Qiwam* (Basic Solution of Particular consistency) of *Chini* (Sugar).

Dose: 5-7gm

JAWARISH-E-KAMOONI

Definition:

Jawarish-e-Kamooni is a semi-solid preparation made with the ingredients in the formulation composition given below:

Formulation composition:

1. *Zeera Siyah*   *(Carum carvi)*   70 gm

2. *Barg-e-Sudab*   *(Ruta graveolens)*   70 gm

3. *Filfil Siyah*   *(Piper nigrum)*   70 gm

4. *Zanjabeel*   *(Zingiber officinale)*   70 gm

5. *Bura-e-Armani* (Silicates of alumina & Iron oxide)   20gm

6. *Qand Safaid*   (Sugar)   1 kg

Method of preparation:

• Take all the ingredients of pharmacopoeial quality.

• Clean, dry and grind the ingredients number 1 to 5, separately and sieve through mesh number 80.

• Dissolve ingredient number 6 in water on slow heat.

• Boil the content and add 0.1% citric acid, while boiling, mix thoroughly and make the quiwam of 78% consistency.

• Remove the vessel from the fire, while hot, add the mixed powders of ingredients number 1 to 5 and mix thoroughly.

• Prepare the homogenous product and allow it to cool.

Actions :

Mujaffif (Desiccant, Siccative), *Jazib* (Absorb efacient) *Kasir-e-Riyah* (Carminative)

Therapeutic uses:

Humuzat-e-Meda (Hyperacidity), *Fuwaq* (Hiccough), *Qeela Maeeya* (Hydroceie), *Nafkh-e-Shikam* (Flatulence in the stomach), *Fataq-e-Urbi* (Inguina Hernia), *Qabz* (Constipation)

Dose 10-15 gm.

QURS MASTAGI

Formulation composition:

Ood Hindi	*(Aquilaria agallocha)*	20 gm.
Mastagi	*(Pistacia lantiscus)*	20 gm.
Post-e-Berun-e-Pista	*(Pistacia vera)*	40 gm.
Gul-e-Surkh	*(Rosa damascena)*	50 gm.
Satt-e-Aamla	*(Emblica officianalis)*	50 gm.

Action:

Daf-e-Qai

Therapeutic use:

Qai. Fuwaq

Dose: 3 to 5 gm

QURS-E-KUNDUR

Formulation composition:

1. Kundur	*(Boswellia serrata)*	8 gm.
2. Rasan	*(Inula racemose)*	10gm.
3. Pudina Khushk	*(Mentha viridis)*	10 gm.
4. Barg-e-Sudab	*(Ruta Graveolens)*	10 gm.
5. Satar Farsi	*(Satureja thymbra)*	5 gm.
6. Nankhwah	*(Trachyspermum ammi)*	5 gm.

Action:

Musakkin

Therapeutic use*:*

Fuwaq, Burudat-e-Meda

Dose: 3 to 5 gm.

QURS-E-SUMAQ MUSHTAHI

Formulation composition:

1. Sumaq	(Rhus coriaria)	30 gm.
2. Zar-e-Ward	(Rosa damascene)	20 gm.
3. Tabasheer	(Bambusa arundinasia)	20 gm.
4. Zeera Siyah	(Carum carvi)	20 gm.
5. Kishneez Khushk	(Coriandrum sativum)	20 gm.
6. Araq-e-Gulab	(Rosa damascena)	20 gm.
7. Post-e-Berun-e-Pista	(Pistaica vera)	20 gm.
8. Mastagi	(Pistacia lentiscus)	10 gm.
9. Araq-e-Gulab	(Rosa damascena)	Q. S.

Action:

Mushtahi, Daf-e-Qai

Therapeutic use:

Zof-e-Ishteha, Qai

Dose: 3 to 5 gm.

HABB-E- ZARANBAD

Formulation composition:

Zaranbad	*(Curcuma Zadoria)*	10 gm.
Araq-e-Gulab	*(Rosa damascena)*	Q. S.

Action:

Daf-e-Safra

Therapeutic use:

Ghasiyan, Qai, Tukhma

Dose: 250mg.

HABB-E-SANA

Formulation composition:

1. *Sana*	*(Casia angustifolia)*	3.5 gm.
2. *Post-e-Halela Kabli*	*(Terminalia Chebula)*	3.5 gm.
3. *Filfil Siyah*	*(Piper nigrum)*	3.5 gm.
4. *Maweez Munaqqa*	*(Vitis vinifera)*	42 gm.
5. *Gul-e-Surkh*	*(Rosa damascena)*	3.5 gm.

Action:

Mulaiyin, kasir-e-Riyah, Hazim

Therapeutic use:

Qabz, Nafkh-e-Shikam, Su-e-Hazm, Qai

Dose: 5 to 10 gm

HABB-E-NARKACHOOR

Formulation composition:

1. *Narkachoor*   (*Zingiber Zurambate*)   200 gm

2. *Pudina Khusk*   (*Mentha viridis*)   200 gm

3. *Ilaichi Khurd*   (*Elettaria cardamomum*)   200 gm

4. *Araq-e-Gulab*   (*Rosa damascena*)   Q.S.

ACTION:

Daf-e-Qai, Daf-e-Ghasiyan

THERAPEUTIC USE:

Qai, Ghasiyan, Awariz-e-Atfal

DOSE: One pill

HABB-E-PAPITA DESI

Definition:

Habb-e-Papita Desi is a solid preparation (pill) made with the ingredients in the formulation composition given below:

Formulation composition:

1. *Papita Desi Khushk*   *(Carica papaya)*   50 gm

2. *Zanjabeel*   *(Zingiber officinale)*   10 gm

3. *Naushadar*   (Sal Ammoniac)   10 gm

4. *Namak-e-Sang*   (Rock Salt)   10 gm

5. *Filfil Siyah*   *(Piper nigrum)*   10 gm

Method of preparation:

• Take all the ingredients of pharmacopoeial quality.

• Powder all the ingredients separately and pass through the sieve of mesh number 80.

• Mix the powders as per Formulation composition and make a semi-solid mass by kneading using minimum quantity of purified water.

• Roll the mass between the fingers to make pill manually to get the pills of 250 mg. from light and dark place.

Actions :

Muqawwi-e-Meda   (Stomachic),   *Kasir-e-Riyah* (Carminative)

Therapeutic uses:

Qabz (Constipation), *Waj-ul-Meda* (Stomachache), *Nafkh-e-Shikam*

(Flatulence)

Dose 1-2 pills after meals

Mode of administration: The drug is taken with water.

MAJOON-E-BHANGRA

Formulation composition:

1. *Filfil Daraz*   *(Piper longum)*   350gm.

2. *Tukhm-e-Panwar*   *(Cassia tora)*   350gm.

3. *Sheetraj Hindi*   *(Plumbago Zeylanica)*   350gm.

4. *Satawar*   *(Asparagus racemosus)*   350gm.

5. *Halela Siyah*   *(Terminalia Chebula)*   350gm.

6. *Balela*   *(Terminalia bellirica)*   350gm.

7. *Bhangra*   *(Eclipta Alba)*   350gm.

8. *Aamla*   *(Emblica officianalis)*   350gm.

9. *Zanjabeel*   *(Zingiber officinale)*   350gm.

10. *Qand Safaid*   (Sugar)   350gm.

Action:

Kasir-e-Riyah

Therapeutic use:

Nafkh-e-Shikam Dafe Qai

Dose: 10 to 20gm

MAJOON-E-SANDAL

Formulation composition:

1. *Sandal Safaid*   (*Santalum album*)   110gm.

2. *Aab-e-Zulal Tamar Hindi* (*Tamarindus indica*)   250ml

3. *Aab-e-Anar Trush* (*Punica granatum*)   350gm

4. *Tabasheer Safaid* (*Bambusa arundinasia*)   15gm

5. *Ood Kham*   (*Aquilaria agallocha*)   15gm.

6. *Zafran*   (*Crocus sativa gynacium*)   5gm.

7. *Qand Safaid*   (Sugar)   750gm.

Action:

Muqawwi-e-meda, Daf-e-safra

Therapeutic use:

Miraq, Qai, Ghasiyan

Dose: 5 to 10gm.

DAWA-E-TATOORA

Formulation composition:

1. *Tukhm-e-Dhatura Siyah (Datura fastusa)*   15gm

2. *Naushadar*   (Sal Ammoniac)   15 gm.

3. *Filfil Siyah*   (*Piper nigrum*)   15 gm.

Method of preparation:

Take all the ingredients of pharmacopoeial quality. Clean and dry all the ingredients except ingredient no. 2 under shade to remove moisture if any. Grind all the ingredients separately, pass through mesh size 60, mix thoroughly and store in tightly closed containers to protect from light and moisture

Action:

Musakkin, Kasir-e-Riyah, Hazim.

Therapeutic use:

Zof-e-Meda, Waj-ul-Meda, Ghasiyan, Qai, Nafkh-e-

Shikam, Su-e-Hazm, Zof-e-Ishteha.

Dose: 60 mg

TIRYAQ-E-MEDA

Definition: Tiryaq-e-Meda is a powdered preparation made with the ingredients given below:

Formulation composition:

1 *Naushadar*	(Ammonium chloride)	10gm
2 *Filfil Siyah*	*(Piper nigrum)*	10gm
3. *Namak-e- Khurdani*	(Sodium chloride)	5gm
4. *Heel Khurd*	*(Elettaria cardamomum)*	5gm

Method of preparation:

- Take all ingredients of pharmacopoeial quality.
- Clean, dry and powder ingredient no. 1 to 4 separately.
- Weigh powdered ingredient, mix together and pass through mesh size 80 to obtain a homogenous blend.
- Store in containers and make them air tight to protect from light and moisture.

Actions: *Hazim* (digestive), *Kasir-e-Riyah* (Carminative)

Therapeutic uses:

Zofe Hazm (Indigestion), *Nafakh-e-Shikam* (Flatulence of the stomach)

Dose: 0.5 – 1gm

Mode of administration: For oral use along with luke-warm water

FAWAKEHEEN

Formulation composition:

1. *Araq-e-Gulab*   *Rosa damascena)*   6 lit

2. *Sirka Neshakar*   (Sugarcain vinegar)   5.25 lit

3. Sharbat-e-Anar *Shireen* *(Punica granatum)*   15 lit

4. *Sharbat-e-*Kamrak   (*Averrhoa carambola*)   9 lit

5. *Sharbat-e-Anar Qandhari (Syrup Punica granatum)*   15lit
15 lit

6. *Qand Safaid*   (Sugar)   51kg

8. *Pudina Sabz*   *Mentha viridis)*   16 kg

ACTION:

Daf-e-Safra, Daf-e-Qai, Hazim, Moharrik-e-Kabid, Moharrik-e-Kulya

THERAPEUTIC USE:

Zof-e-Ishteha, Zof-e-Kabid wa Kulya, Su-e-Hazm, Qai, Ghisyan

DOSE: 10-20 ml after meals

NAUJIVAN GHUTTI

Formulation composition:

1. *Badiyan*	*(Foeniculum vulgare)*	500 gm
2. *Gul-e-Surkh*	*(Rosa damascena)*	750 gm
3. *Naushadar*	(Ammonium chloride)	125 gm
4. *Narkachoor*	*(Zingiber Zurambate)*	250 gm
5. *Maghz-e-Amaltas*	*(Casia fistula)*	250 gm
6. *Ajwayin Desi*	*(Trachyspermum ammi)*	250 gm
7. *Baobarang*	*(Embelia ribe)*	250 gm
8. *Sibr-e-Zard*	*(Aloe barbadensis)*	125 gm
9. *Barg-e-Sana-e-Makkai*	*(Casia angustifolia)*	250 gm
10. *Atees Shireen*	*(Aconitum hetrophyllum)*	250 gm
11. *Unnab Wilayeti*	*(Ziziphus Jujuba)*	250 gm
12. *Gilo Sabz*	*(Tinospora cordifolia)*	250 gm
13. *Hilteet Khalis*	*(Ferula foetida)*	125 gm
14. *Kakra Singhi*	*(Pistacia integerrima)*	250 gm
15. *Namak Siyah*	(Black Salt)	250 gm

16. *Zanjabeel*	*(Zingiber officinale)*	250 gm
17. *Chaksu*	*(Cassia absus)*	250 gm
18. *Halela Zard*	*(Terminalia Chebula)*	250 gm
19. *Heel Kalan*	*(Amomum subulatum)*	250 gm
20. *Qand Safaid*	(Sugar)	47.50 Kg

ACTION:

Daf-e-Humma, Daf-e-Qai, Qabiz, Mulaiyin

THERAPEUTIC USE:

Nazla, Zukam, Sual, Su-e-Hazm, Is-hal, Qai, Qabz

DOSE:

Upto 3 month children - 5 drops with mother's milk or water twice a day

3-6 month children - 10 drops with mother's milk or water twice a day.

In case of *Qabz* - increase dose and give with warm water.

SIKANJABEEN- E-LEEMUN

Formulation composition:

1. *Aab-e-Leemu*	(Juice *Citrus lemon*)	750 ml.
2. Sirka Desi	(Vinegar)	300 ml
. 3. *Shakar safaid*	(Sugar)	4 kg.
4. *Sat lemon*	(Extract *Citrus lemon*)	12 gm.
5. *Aab*	(Water)	500 ml.

ACTION: *Daf-e-Tap Daf-e-Qai*

THERAPEUTIC USE: *In Hummiyat-e-Safraviah, Qai, Matli and Shiddat-e-Atash.*

DOSE: 25 ml

NAUSEA AND VOMITING

(Modern Concept)

As per the modern concept vomiting is co-ordinated by the brain stem and is effected by neuro-muscular responses in the gut, pharynx, and thoraco-abdominal wall. The mechanisms underlying nausea are poorly understood but likely involve the cerebral cortex, as nausea requires conscious perception. Electro-encephalographic studies show activation of temporo-frontal cortical regions with induction of nausea. brain stem nuclei initiate emesis, including the nucleus tractus solitarius, the dorsal vagal and phrenic nuclei, and medullary nuclei that regulate respiration; nuclei that control pharyngeal, facial, and tongue movements co-ordinate the initiation of emesis. The neuro transmitters involved in this coordination are uncertain; however, roles for neurokinin, serotonin, and vasopressin pathways are postulated. Somatic and visceral muscles exhibit stereotypic responses during vomiting. Inspiratory thoracic and abdominal wall muscles contract, producing high intra-thoracic and intra-abdominal pressures that facilitate expulsion of gastric contents. The gastric cardia herniates across the diaphragm, and the larynx moves upward to promote oral propulsion of the vomitus. Under normal conditions, distally migrating gut contractions are regulated by an electrical phenomenon, the slow wave which cycles at 3 cycles/min in the stomach and eleven cycles/min in the duodenum. With vomiting, slow waves are replaced by orally propagating spike activity, which induces retrograde contractions that assist in the oral expulsion of small-intestinal contents.

Activators of Emesis

Emetic stimuli act at several anatomic sites. Emesis provoked by noxious thoughts or smells originates in the cerebral cortex, whereas cranial nerves mediate vomiting after gag reflex activation. Motion sickness and inner ear disorders act on the labyrinthine apparatus, while gastric irritants and emetogenic anti-cancer agents such as cisplatin stimulate gastroduodenal vagal afferent nerves. Non gastric visceral afferents are activated by small intestinal and colonic obstruction and mesenteric ischemia. The area postrema, a medullary nucleus, responds to blood borne emetic stimuli and is termed the chemo-receptor trigger zone. Many emetic drugs act on the area postrema as do bacterial toxins and metabolic disorders such as uremia, hypoxia, and ketoacidosis. Neuro-transmitters that mediate induction of vomiting are selective for these anatomic sites. Labyrinthine disorders stimulate vestibular cholinergic muscarinic M1 and histaminergic H1 receptors, whereas gastroduodenal vagal afferent stimuli activate serotonin 5-HT3 receptors. The area postrema is richly served by nerve fibers acting on 5HT3, M1, H1, and dopamine D2 receptor subtypes. Optimal pharmacologic management requires an understanding of these pathways.

CAUSES OF NAUEA AND VOMATING:

Intraperitoneal	Extra peritoneal	Medications/Metabolic Disorders
Obstructing disorder like Pyloric Obstruction Small bowel obstruction Colonic Obstruction Superior mesenteric artery syndrome	Cardiopulmonary Disease Cardiomyopathy Myocardial infection	Drugs Cancer chemotherapy Antibiotics Cardiac anti - arrhythmic Digoxin Oral hypo glycaemic Oral contraceptives
Enteric infections Viral and Bacterial	Labyrinthine disease Motion sickness Labyrinthitis Malignancy	Endocrine/metabolic disease Pregnancy Uremia Ketoacidosis Thyroid and parathyroid disease, Adrenal insufficiency
Inflammatory diseases like Cholecystitis Pancreatitis Appendicitis Hepatitis	Intracerebral disorders Malignancy Haemorrhage Abscess Hydrocephalus	Toxins Liver failure Ethanol

Impaired motor function like	Psychiatric illness	
Gastroparesis Intestinal pseudo-obstruction Functional Dyspepsia Gastroesophageal. reflux	Anorexia and bulimia nervosa Depression Psychogenic vomiting	
Biliary colic Abdominal irradiation	Postoperative vomiting Cyclic vomiting syndrome	

TREATMENT

General Principles

Therapy of vomiting is tailored to correction of medically or surgically remediable abnormalities, if possible. Hospitalization is considered for severe dehydration, especially if oral fluid replenishment cannot be sustained. Once oral intake is tolerated, nutrients are restarted with liquids that are low in fat, as lipids delay gastric emptying. Foods high in indigestible residues are avoided because these also prolong gastric retention.

ANTIEMETIC MEDICATION

The most commonly used anti-emetic agents act on the central nervous system. Anti-histamines such as meclizine and dimenhydrinate and anticholinergic drugs such as scopolamine act on labyrinthine-activated pathways and are use full in motion sickness and inner ear disorders. Phenothiazine and butyrophenone dopamine D2 antagonists are used to treat emesis evoked by area postrema stimuli and are effective for medication, toxic, and metabolic aetiologies. Dopamine antagonists freely cross the blood-brain barrier and may cause anxiety, dystonic reactions, hyper pro lactinemic effects, and irreversible tardive dyskinesia. Other drug classes have antiemetic properties. Serotonin 5-HT3 antagonists such as ondansetron and granisetron are useful in the treatment of postoperative vomiting, after radiation therapy, and in the prevention of cancer chemotherapy–induced emesis. The usefulness of 5-

HT3 antagonists for other causes of emesis is less well established. Low-dose tricyclic antidepressants provide symptomatic benefit inpatients with unexplained nausea of a functional nature, as well as in diabetic patients with nausea and vomiting whose disease is of long standing.

Gastrointestinal Motor Stimulants

Drugs that stimulate gastric emptying are indicated for gastroparesis. Metoclopramide, a combined 5-HT4 agonist and D2 antagonist, is effective in gastroparesis, but anti dopaminergic side effects limit its use in 20% of patients. Erythromycin, a macrolide antibiotic, potently increases gastroduodenal motility by action on receptors for motilin, an endogenous stimulant of fasting motor activity. Intravenous erythromycin is useful in patients with refractory gastroparesis; however, oral forms of the drug also have some effect. Domperidone, a D2 antagonist not available in the United States, has pro kinetic and antiemetic effects but does not cross into most other brain regions; thus, anxiety and dystonic reactions are rare. The main side effects of Domperidone are induction of hyperprolactinemia through effects on pituitary regions served by a porous blood-brain barrier. Patients with refractory upper gut motility disorders pose significant challenges. Liquid suspensions of pro kinetic drugs may be beneficial as liquids empty from the stomach more rapidly than pills. Metoclopramide can be administered subcutaneously in patients who do not respond to oral drugs. Intestinal pseudo obstruction may respond to the somatostatin analogue octreotide, which induces propagative small-intestinal motor complexes. Pyloric injections of botulinum toxin are reported in uncontrolled studies to benefit patients with idiopathic or diabetic gastroparesis. Placement of a feeding jejunostomy reduces hospitalizations and improves overall health in some patients with gastroparesis who do not respond to drug therapy. Surgical options are limited for refractory cases, but post vagotomy gastroparesis may improve with near-total resection of the stomach. Implanted gastric electrical pace-makers and neuro stimulators may reduce symptoms, improve quality-of-life, and decrease health care expenditures in patients with medication-refractory gastroparesis.

Cancer chemotherapeutic agents such as cisplatin are intensely emetogenic. Given prophylactically, 5-HT3 antagonists prevent chemotherapy-induced acute vomiting in most cases. Optimal antiemetic effects are often obtained with a 5HT3 antagonist in combination with a glucocorticoid. High-dose metoclopramide is also effective in chemotherapy-evoked emesis, whereas benzodiazepines such as lorazepam are useful in reducing anticipatory nausea and vomiting. Delayed emesis 1 to 5 days after chemotherapy is more refractory to treatment. Novelneurokinin NK1 antagonists may be potent antiemetic and anti-nausea drugs during both the acute and the delayed periods after chemotherapy. Cannabinoids such as tetra-hydro-cannabinol, long advocated for cancer-associated emesis, produce significant side effects and are no more effective than anti-dopaminergic agents. Most current drug regimens are more effective at controlling emesis than nausea. The clinician should exercise caution in managing the pregnant patient with nausea. Studies of the teratogenic effects of available antiemetic agents provide conflicting results. Few controlled trials have been performed in the nausea of pregnancy, although antihistamines such as meclizine and anti dopaminergics such as prochlorperazineare more effective than placebo. Alternative therapies such as pyridoxine, acupressure, or ginger are being tested. Controlling emesis in children with cyclic vomiting syndrome is a challenge. 5-HT3 antagonists are a mainstay of treatment. Considering the possible link to migraine headaches, anti-migraine therapy with anti-depressants and the serotonin 5-HT1 agonist, sumatriptan, may be tried.

VOMITING IN PREGNANCY

The vomiting is related to the pregnant state and depending upon the severity, it is classified as:

(i) Simple vomiting of pregnancy or milder type

(ii) Hyperemesis gravidarum or severe type.

SIMPLE VOMITING

(Syn: morning sickness, emesis gravidarum):

The patient complains of nausea and occasional sickness on rising in the morning. Slight vomiting is so common in early pregnancy (about 50%) that it is considered as a symptom of pregnancy. It may, however, occur at other times of the day. The vomitus is small and clear or bile stained. It does not produce any impairment of health or restrict the normal activities of the women. The feature disappears with or without treatment by 12-14th week of pregnancy. High level of serum human chorionic gonadotropin, estrogen and altered immunological states are considered responsible for initiation of the manifestation, which is probably aggravated by the neurogenic factor.

Management:

Assurance is important. Taking of dry toast or biscuit and avoidance of fatty and spicy foods are enough to relieve the symptoms in majority. If the simple measures fail, antiemetic drugs — trifluoperazine (Espazine) 1 mg twice daily and phenobarbitone 30-60 mg tab at bed time are quite effective. Patient is advised to take plenty of fluids (2.5 L in 24 hours) and fruit juice.

TREATMENT OF NAUSEA AND VOMITING:

Treatment	Mechanism	Examples	Clinical Indications
Antiemetic agents	Antihistaminergic	Dimenhydrinate, meclizine	Motion sickness, inner ear disease
	Anticholinergic	Scopolamine	Motion sickness, inner ear disease
	Antidopaminergic	Prochlorperazin, droperidol	Medication, toxin-, or metabolic-induced emesis
	5-HT3 antagonist	Ondansetron, granisetron	Chemotherp-y and radiation induced emesis, postoperative emesis
	Tricyclic antidepressant	Amitriptyline, nortriptyline	Functional nausea

ANTIEMETICS

These are drugs used to prevent or suppress vomiting.

CLASSIFICATION

1. **Anticholinergics**
   Hyoscine, Dicyclomine
2. **H1 antihistaminics**
   Promethazine, Diphenhydramine, Dimenhydrinate, Doxylamine, Cyclizine, Meclozine, Cinnarizine.
3. **Neuroleptics Chlorpromazine, (D2 blockers)**
   Prochlorperazine, Haloperidol, etc.
4. **Prokinetic drugs**
   Metoclopramide, Domperidone, Cisapride, Mosapride Tegaserod
5. **5-HT3 antagonists** Ondansetron, Granisetron
6. **Adjuvant**
   Dexamethasone, antiemetics Benzodiazepines, Cannabinoids.

ANTICHOLINERGICS:
1) **Hyoscine**
2) **Dicyclomine**

Hyoscine

Hyoscine is the most effective drug for motion sickness. However, it has a brief duration of action; produces sedation and other anticholinergic side effects; suitable only for short brisk journies. It acts probably by blocking conduction of nerve impulses across a cholinergic link in the pathway leading from the vestibular apparatus to the vomiting centre and is not effective in vomiting of other etiologies. A transdermal patch containing 1.5 mg of hyoscine, to be delivered over 3 days has been developed. Applied behind the pinna, it suppresses motion sickness while producing only mild side effects.
Dose (0.2–0.4 mg oral, i.m.)

Dicyclomine
Dose (10–20 mg oral) has been used for prophylaxis of motion sickness and for morning sickness. It has been cleared of teratogenic potential.

H1 ANTIHISTAMINICS

Some antihistaminics are antiemetic. They are useful mainly in motion sickness and to a lesser extent in morning sickness, postoperative and some other forms of vomiting. Their antiemetic effect appears to be based on anticholinergic, antihistaminic and sedative properties.

Promethazine

Diphenhydramine

dimenhydrinate

These drugs afford protection of motion sickness for 4–6 hours, but produce sedation and dryness of mouth. By their central anticholinergic action, they block the extrapyramidal side effects of metoclopramide while supplementing its anti-emetic action. Their combination is used in chemotherapy induced vomiting.

Promethazine theoclate

Promethazine theoclate. It has been specially promoted as an antiemetic, but the action does not appear to be significantly different from promethazine HCl.

Brand Names AVOMINE 25 mg.

Doxylamine

It is a sedative H1 antihistaminic with prominent anticholinergic activity. Marketed in combination with pyridoxine, it is specifically promoted in India for 'morning sickness' (vomiting of early pregnancy) although such use is not made in the USA, UK and many other countries. Oral absorption of doxylamine is slow, and its t½ is 10 hr. The side effects are drowsiness, dry mouth, vertigo and abdominal upset. Dose: 10–20 mg at bed time; if needed additional doses may be given in morning and afternoon.

Brand Names
DOXINATE,
GRAVIDOX,
VOMNEX,
NOSIC: 10 mg with pyridoxine 10 mg tab.

Cyclizine, meclizine

These are less sedative and less anticholinergic. Meclizine is long-acting, protects against sea sickness for nearly 24 hours.

Brand Names
Cyclizine 50 mg tab;
DILIGAN: Meclizine 12.5 mg + nicotinic acid 50 mg tab;
PREGNIDOXIN: Meclizine 25 mg + Caffeine 20 mg tab.

Cinnarizine

It is an antivertigo drug, and is also protective for motion sickness. It probably acts by inhibiting influx of $Ca2+$ from endolymph into the vestibular sensory cells which mediates labyrinthine reflexes. Anticholinergic-antihistaminic antiemetics are the first choice drugs for motion sickness. Antidopaminergic and anti-HT3 drugs are less effective. All antimotion sickness drugs act better when taken ½–1 hour before commencing journey. Once sickness has started, it is more difficult to control; higher doses/parenteral administration may be needed. The antihistaminics are suspected to have teratogenic potential, but there is no conclusive proof. Nevertheless, it is better to avoid them for morning sickness. Most cases of morning sickness can be managed by reassurance and dietary adjustment. If an antiemetic has to be used, dicyclomine, promethazine, prochlorperazine or metoclopramide may be prescribed in low doses.

NEUROLEPTICS

These are potent antiemetics; act by blocking D2 receptors in the CTZ; antagonize apomorphine induced vomiting and have additional antimuscarinic as well as H1 antihistaminic property. They have broad spectrum antiemetic action effective in: Drug induced and postanaesthetic nausea and vomiting. Disease induced vomiting: gastroenteritis, uraemia, liver disease, migraine, etc. Malignancy associated and cancer chemotherapy (mildly emetogenic) induced vomiting. Radiation sickness vomiting (less effective). Morning sickness: should not be used except in hyperemesis gravidarum.

They are less effective in motion sickness: the pathway does not involve dopaminergic link. Most of these drugs produce significant degree of sedation. Acute muscle dystonia may occur after a single dose, especially in children and girls. The antiemetic dose is generally much lower than antipsychotic doses. These agents should not be administered until the cause of vomiting has been diagnosed; otherwise specific treatment of conditions like intestinal obstruction, appendicitis may be delayed due to symptom relief.

Prochlorperazine

This D2 blocking phenothiazine is a labyrinthine suppressant, has selective antivertigo and antiemetic actions. It is highly effective when given by injection in vertigo associated with vomiting and to some extent in cancer chemotherapy associated vomiting. Prochlorperazine is used as an antiemetic rather than as antipsychotic.

Muscle dystonia and other extrapyramidal side effects are the most important limiting features.

Brand Name

STEMETIL 5, 25 mg tabs., 12.5 mg/ml inj, 1 ml amp, 10 ml vial

PROKINETIC DRUGS

1) **Metoclopramide**
2) **Domperidone**
3) **Cisapride**
4) **Mosapride**
5) **Tegaserod**

These are drugs which promote gastrointestinal transit and speed gastric emptying by enhancing coordinated propulsive motility.

Metoclopramide

Metoclopramide is chemically related to procainamide, but has no pharmacological similarity with it. Introduced in early 1970s as a 'gastric hurrying' agent, it is now a widely used antiemetic.

Dose:

10 mg (children 0.2–0.5 mg/kg) TDS oral or i.m. For chemotherapy induced vomiting 0.3–1.0 mg/kg slow i.v./i.m.

Brand Name

PERINORM,

MAXERON,

REGLAN,

SIGMET, 10 mg tab; 5 mg/5 ml syr; 10 mg/2 ml inj.; 50 mg/ 10 ml inj.

Uses.

Antiemetic: Metoclopramide is an effective and popular drug for many types of vomiting— postoperative, drug induced, disease associated (especially migraine), radiation sickness, etc, but is less effective in motion sickness. Though ondansetron is preferred, metoclopramide continues to be used for prophylaxis and treatment of vomiting induced by highly emetic anticancer drugs (cisplatin, etc.). A higher dose (1 mg/kg i.v.) is often needed, but is effective when phenothiazines and antihistamines do not work. Promethazine, diphenhydramine, diazepam or lorazepam injected i.v. along with metoclopramide supplement its antiemetic action and reduce the attending dystonic reactions. Dexamethasone i.v. also augments the efficacy of metoclopramide. Though no teratogenic effects have been reported, metoclopramide should be used for morning sickness only when not controlled by other measures.

Domperidone

It is a D2 antagonist, chemically related to haloperidol, but pharmacologically related to metoclopramide. It has lower ceiling antiemetic and prokinetic actions. Unlike metoclopramide, its prokinetic action is not blocked by atropine and is based only on D2 receptor blockade in upper g.i.t. Domperidone crosses blood-brain barrier poorly. Accordingly, extrapyramidal side effects are rare, but hyperprolactinaemia can occur. However, it does act on CTZ which is not protected by blood-brain barrier. Antiemetic efficacy is lower than metoclopramide. Administered with levodopa or bromocriptine, it counteracts their dose limiting emetic action without affecting the therapeutic effect in parkinsonism. Domperidone is absorbed orally, but bioavailability is only ~15% due to first pass metabolism. It is completely biotransformed and metabolites are excreted in urine. Plasma $t\frac{1}{2}$ is 7.5 hr.

Side effects

Side effects are much less than with metoclopramide: dry mouth, loose stools, headache, rashes, galactorrhoea. Cardiac arrhythmias have developed on rapid i.v. injection.

Dose: 10–40 mg (Children 0.3–0.6 mg/kg) TDS.

Brand Name

DOMSTAL, DOMPERON, NORMETIC 10 mg tab, 1 mg/ml susp,

MOTINORM 10 mg tab, 10 mg/ml drops.

Cisapride

It is a prokinetic drug with little antiemetic property, because it lacks D2 receptor antagonism. Effects of cisapride on gastric motility resemble metoclopramide—gastric emptying is accelerated, LES tone is improved and esophageal peristalsis is augmented. It restores and facilitates motility throughout the g.i.t., including colon (metoclopramide/domperidone do not accelerate colonic transit). It has been withdrawn in USA and some other countries, but is available in India.

Dose: 10–20 mg TDS;

Brand Name

SYSPRIDE, UNIPRIDE, NUPRIDE 10 mg tab;

MOTEN,

PULSID 10 mg tab, 5 mg/5 ml susp.;

CIZA also 20 mg tab

Mosapride

A newer congener of cisapride with similar gastrokinetic and LES tonic action due to 5-HT4 agonistic (major) and 5-HT3 antagonistic (minor) action in the myenteric plexus, but has not caused Q-Tc prolongation or arrhythmias. Like cisapride, it has no clinically useful antiemetic action and does not produce extrapyramidal/hyperprolactinaemic side effects due to absence of D2 blocking property.

Indications and side effects are similar to cisapride.

Dose: 5 mg (elderly 2.5 mg) TDS.

Brand Name

MOZA, MOZASEF, NORMAGUT 2.5, mg, 5 mg tabs;

MOZA MPS: 5 mg + methylpolysiloxane 125 mg tab.

Tegaserod

It is a recently introduced selective 5-HT4 partial agonist, with no action on 5-HT3 and other receptors, which mainly augments colonic motility along with promotion of gastric emptying and intestinal transit, and less effect on LES tone. The 5-HT4 agonistic action also increases colonic Cl– (and water) secretion. The current indication of tegaserod is constipation predominant irritable bowel syndrome. Its possible use as a gastrokinetic is being explored.

5-HT3 ANTAGONISTS:

Ondansetron

It is the prototype of a new class of antiemetic drugs developed to control cancer chemotherapy/radiotherapy induced vomiting, and later found to be highly effective in postoperative nausea and vomiting as well. It blocks the depolarizing action of 5-HT through 5-HT3 receptors on vagal afferents in the g.i.t. as well as in NTS and CTZ. Cytotoxic drugs/ radiation produce nausea and vomiting by causing cellular damage → release of mediators including 5-HT from intestinal mucosa → activation of vagal afferents in the gut → emetogenic impulses to the NTS and CTZ. Ondansetron blocks emetogenic impulses both at their peripheral origin and their central relay. It does not block dopamine receptors and apomorphine or motion sickness induced vomiting. A weak gastrokinetic action due to 5-HT3 blockade has been detected, but it is clinically insignificant. A minor 5-HT4 antagonistic action has also been shown.

Pharmacokinetics:

Oral bioavailability of ondansetron is 60–70% due to first pass metabolism. It is hydroxylated by CYP 1A2, 2D6 and 3A, but no clinically significant drug interactions have been noted. It is eliminated in urine and faeces, mostly as metabolites; t½ being 3–5 hrs, and duration of action 4–12 hr. Dose and efficacy: For cisplatin and other highly emetogenic drugs—8 mg i.v. by slow injection over 15 min ½ hr before chemotherapeutic infusion, followed by 2 similar doses 4 hour apart. To prevent delayed emesis 8 mg oral is given twice a day for 3–5 days. For postoperative nausea/vomiting 4–8 mg i.v. given before induction is repeated 8 hourly. For less emetogenic drugs and for radiotherapy an oral dose of 8 mg is given 1–2 hr prior to the procedure and repeated twice 8 hrly. It is effective in 60–80% cases; similar to or better than high doses of metoclopramide, and does not cause dystonias or sedation like the latter.

Barand Name:

 EMESET, VOMIZ, OSETRON, EMSETRON 4,8 mg tabs, 2 mg/ml inj in 2 ml and 4 ml amps.

Patients who do not obtain optimum protection by ondansetron alone, addition of dexamethasone, promethazine/diazepam or both enhances antiemetic efficacy. Adjuvant drugs are more often required for delayed phase vomiting that occurs on the second to fourth day of cisplatin therapy, because 5-HT3 antagonists alone are less effective. Other types of vomiting: Efficacy of 5-HT3 antagonists in prevention and treatment of postoperative nausea and vomiting is now well established. Since this vomiting is multifactorial in origin, 5-HT3 blockers are not as completely efficacious as in chemotherapy induced vomiting, and many other classes of antiemetic drugs are also protective. In comparative trials, superiority of ondansetron in terms of efficacy as well as lack of side effects and drug interactions has been demonstrated. Administered before surgery ondansetron (4–8 mg i.v.) repeated after 4 hours has become the first choice antiemetic at many centres. Reports of efficacy in vomiting associated with drug overdosage, side effect of cotrimoxazole and fluvoxamine, uraemia and certain neurological injuries are also available. Some 5-HT3 antagonists have produced symptomatic relief in diarrhoea-predominant irritable bowel syndrome. Side effects: Ondansetron is generally well tolerated: the only common side effect is headache. Mild constipation or diarrhoea and abdominal discomfort occur in few patients. Rashes and allergic reactions are reported, especially after i.v. injection.

<h1 style="text-align:center">Granisetron</h1>

It is 10–15 times more potent than ondansetron and probably more effective during the repeat cycle of chemotherapy. The weak 5-HT4 blockade seen in ondansetron has not been detected in granisetron. Its plasma t½ is longer (8–12 hrs) and it needs to be given only twice on the day of chemotherapy. Side effect profile is similar to ondansetron.

Dose:

10 μg/kg i.v. 30 min before chemotherapy, repeated after 12 hr. For less emetogenic regimen 2 mg oral 1 hr before chemotherapy or 1 mg before and 1 mg 12 hr after it.

Brand Name

GRANICIP, GRANISET 1 mg, 2 mg tabs; 1 mg/ml inj. (1, 3 ml amps).

Dolasetron, Tropisetron, and Palonasetron are the other selective 5-HT3 antagonists.

ADJUVANT ANTIEMETICS

<h3 style="text-align:center">Corticosteroids</h3>

(e.g. dexamethasone 8–20 mg i.v.) can alleviate nausea and vomiting due to moderately emetogenic chemotherapy, but are more often employed to augment the efficacy of other primary antiemetic drugs like metoclopramide and ondansetron for highly emetogenic regimens and for cisplatin induced delayed emesis. They also serve to reduce certain side effects of the primary antiemetic. However, because of their metabolic effects, they should be used only in selected and refractory cases.

Benzodiazepines

The weak antiemetic property of BZDs is primarily based on the sedative action. Used as adjuvant to metoclopramide/ondansetron, diazepam/ lorazepam (oral/i.v.) help by relieving anxiety, anticipatory vomiting and produce amnesia for the unpleasant procedure. They also suppress dystonic side effects of metoclopramide.

Cannabinoids and Tetrahydrocannabinol

Cannabinoids and Tetrahydrocannabinol is the active principle of the hallucinogen Cannabis indica. It possesses antiemetic activity against moderately emetogenic chemotherapy. It probably acts at higher centres or at vomiting centre itself by activating CB1 subtype of cannabinoid receptors.

Dronabinol

Dronabinol has been used for chemotherapy induced vomiting in patients who cannot tolerate other antiemetics or are unresponsive to them. It has also been tried as an appetite stimulant in cachectic/AIDS patients. Nabilone is another cannabinoid with antiemetic property

Bibliography

- Akseer-e-Azam. New Delhi: Idara Kitab-us-shifa; 2011

- Al-Akseer. Volume 1st.Delhi: Ijaz publishing House Delhi;2003.

- Kita al-qanoon fi al-tib (Urdu translation by Ghulam Hasnain Kantoori). New Delhi: Idara Kitab-us-Shifa; 2011.

- Moaljat Shar-e-Asbab.1st edition. Delhi. Idara Kitab-us-Shifa; 2009.

- Almoaljat-ul-Buqratiya. Vol. III. New Delhi: CCRUM New Delhi;1997

- Biyaz-e-Azmal. 1st edition. Delhi: Ijaz publishing House Delhi; 2010.

- Harrisons Principle of Internal Medicine.16th edition. New York: Mc Graw-Hill Medical Publishing Division New York; 2005.

- The Unani pharmacopoeia of India. Part I. Volume 1 to Volume 5th New Delhi; Ministry of Health and Family Welfare, Department of Ayurveda, Yoga & Naturopathy, Unani, Siddha and Homoeopathy (Ayush), Government of India; 2009.

- Makhzan-ul-Mufradat (Kitab-ul-Advia). 2nd edition. Delhi: Idara kitab-us-shifa; 2010.

- Minhaj-ul-Elaj.New Delhi; CCRUM, Ministry of AYUSH, Govt. of India New Delhi; 2008.

- National formulary of Unani Medicine.Part–II.Vol.2 to 4th. New Delhi: Ministry of Health and Family Welfare, Govt. of India; 2007.

- Kitab Al-Murakkabat.Aligrh: Ibne sina Academy;2010.

- Anonymous. National formulary of Unani Medicine. part -III,1st edition, New Delhi: CCRUM, Ministry of Health and family welfare. Govt. of India; 2001:7,110,141,149.

- Kabiruddin M. Alqarabadeen.2nd edition. New Delhi: CCRUM, Ministry of Health and family welfare. Govt. of India; 2006:97-98.

- Makhzan-e-Mufradat wa Murakbat. New Delhi: CCRUM, Ministry of Health and family welfare Govt. of India ;2007.

- Al-Qarabadeen. 1st volume. 1st edition. Faislabad: Malik sons.

- Anonymous. Qarabadeen-e-Majeedi. New Delhi: All India Tibbi conference; 1986.

- Khazain-ul-Adviya. New Delhi: Idara Kitab-us-Shifa.

- Minhajus saidla wa al kimiya. New Delhi: Idara Kitabus shifa; 2001.

- Biyaz-e-Kabeer. Haydrabad: Hikmat book dipu.

- Qarabadeen-e-Azam. New Delhi: Ijaz publishing House Delhi; 1996.

- Makhzan-ul-Murakbat.New Delhi:Ijaz publishing House New Delhi.

- Qarabadeen e azam wa akmal. New Delhi: CCRUM; 2005.
- The Encyclopaedia of Medicinal Plants. DK publishing Book, New York;1996.
- Bustan al-mufradat. New Delhi: Idara Kitab-us-Shifa; 2002.
- Taj-ul-Mufaradat (Khawas-ul-Adviya).1st edition. New Delhi:Idara Kitabus shifa New Delhi.2010.
- Indian medicinal plants. New Delhi: Springer (India) Privet Limited; 2007.
- The Useful Plants of India. New Delhi: National Institute of Science Communication and Information Resource; 2006.
- Biyaz-e-Khas.New Delhi: Ijaz Publishing House,New Delhi;2006.
- Qarabadeen-e-Qadri. CCRUM, NewDelhi;2009.
- Hamdard pharmacopoeia of eastern medicine. Delhi: Sri Satguru Publications; 1997.
- Kitabul-Mufradat. International printing press Aligarh; 2001.
- Unani Adviya Mufarrada.10th edition. New Delhi: Qaumi Council Farog-e-Urdu; 2004.